Life With The Holy Spirit

Janet L. Williams

Dedication

I dedicate this book to the Holy Spirit. Every time I think about anything going on with me, the first thing I think of is the Holy Spirit, who comforts me wherever I hurt or counsels me in my heart. He is the reason I'm writing this book.

Acknowledgments

To the man I love (Melvin Labat) and all the years we had before Hurricane Katrina, you are a gift from God. You didn't know you brought richness to my life, and I still get weak in the knees.

To Michael Williams, my son, and my two grandbabies, Rea and MJ Jr. They are all gifts from God and my blessings. Thank you, Rhecia Williams, their mother, because without you, it wouldn't be possible.

About the Author

Janet is a resilient and accomplished individual who has overcome adversity to achieve her dreams. In 1991, a life-altering accident set her on a path of discovery and growth. Years later, in 2011, she became a certified personal trainer, leveraging her passion for fitness to inspire others. Notably, Janet was certified by the renowned 8X Mr. Universe, Lee Haney, in personal training—demonstrating her expertise and dedication in the field.

Janet's writing journey began with her debut book, *Changes*, born out of a divine prompt from the Holy Spirit. Her second book, *Actions for Jesus' Help*, further solidifies her commitment to spreading hope and encouragement.

A dedicated professional, Janet holds numerous certificates of achievement in personal training, bodybuilding, small business management, anatomy, and physiology. She has also been an active member of the Toastmasters International Leadership Club since 2015.

When not writing or training, Janet enjoys sharing the Word and spending time with her beloved grandchildren, Rea and Michael Jr. (MJ). Her story highlights the strength of perseverance, faith, and the pursuit of one's passions.

Preface

This book is the result of a deeply personal journey I have taken with the Holy Spirit. Over the years, I have realized that the Holy Spirit is not a distant or abstract concept but a constant presence guiding me through life. From moments of joy to times of great challenge, I have felt His counsel, comfort, and strength. As Jesus said in John 14:26, *"But the Helper, the Holy Spirit, whom the Father will send in My name, He will teach you all things, and bring to your remembrance all that I said to you."* Through writing this book, I aim to share the impact that living with the Holy Spirit has had on my life and to encourage others to invite Him into theirs.

I have combined personal experiences, biblical teachings, and practical guidance in these pages to help readers develop a closer relationship with the Holy Spirit. I hope you will find inspiration, clarity, and support as you explore your spiritual journey. Each chapter offers insight into the ways the Holy Spirit works within us—whether offering comfort in difficult times, helping us grow in faith, or empowering us to use our God-given gifts to serve others.

One of the main messages of this book is that the Holy Spirit is accessible to everyone, regardless of where they are in their spiritual journey. Whether you are new to your faith or have been walking with God for many years, the Holy Spirit is eager to guide, heal, and strengthen you. I encourage you to approach this book with an open heart, ready to receive the wisdom and comfort the Holy Spirit can provide.

I am grateful to the Holy Spirit for the inspiration and guidance that made this book possible. As you read these words, I hope you will feel the same peace, comfort, and sense of purpose that I have experienced through my relationship with the Holy Spirit. May this book serve as a companion and guide as you walk the path of faith, knowing that the Holy Spirit is with you every step.

Contents

Introduction

Welcome to a journey that will revolutionize your view of religion, Jesus Christ, and the Holy Spirit. "LIFE WITH THE HOLY SPIRIT," a passionate guide to a more meaningful spiritual existence, is more than just a compilation of religious concepts.

Consider embarking on a path closer to inner peace and liberation. You can do that with the Holy Spirit. It's about finding love without conditions, tranquility beyond comprehension, and joy beyond words. I'm excited to share the Holy Spirit's miracles and beauty on this journey that will change your life. If you want to deepen your faith, this book is perfect for you, whether you're 13-18 or 18-24, and so on. It's full of inspiration and guidance.

Like many, my relationship with the Holy Spirit began as a youngster, when I sometimes felt hollow around family and friends. Space seemed unfilled, and my contact with the Holy Spirit altered everything. After going on that path, I can't describe my inner calm and security, as it changed me and inspired me to learn and grow spiritually.

This book will contain more of my opinions and experiences; though I am not an expert, I am a fellow pilgrim on this religious journey. These stories demonstrate the Holy Spirit's fantastic work in your life. This book is a friend and companion you can come to for support, direction, or a reminder of God's love.

Each chapter in this book is deliberately designed to build on the previous one and provide thorough guidance to Holy Spirit-led living. First, we'll discuss salvation and Christian living. This fundamental information sets the stage for everything else. We must know how we were rescued to grasp the Holy Spirit's action in our lives and the Holy Spirit's function in our lives as we go. This session will cover the fruits, talents, and ways to become closer to the Holy Spirit through daily worship and prayer. Each chapter's practical advice, biblical truths, and personal experiences can be applied to your life.

This journey is about learning and changing things. The Holy Spirit is a natural person whom we can trust every day to comfort, guide, and teach us. This book should make the Holy Spirit less mysterious and show how easy it is to connect with Him and how vital He is to your life.

This work should be read with an open heart and mind. Prepare to challenge your beliefs, grow, and innovate. This is a Holy Spirit-filled reading. Read each chapter, pray, and ask the Holy Spirit for guidance. Let Him speak to you and reveal Himself in fresh ways.

As we embark, remember you are not alone. Christians help and pray for each other; many others are treading this route with you. Our connection to the Holy Spirit is unbreakable. Working together lets us learn, grow, and live out God's plan for our lives.

Personal Story: My Journey with the Holy Spirit

As a teen, I often wondered, "Who am I? What is my purpose? Do you believe in God? Is He concerned about me?" It was hard to ask questions from my mind and heart, which made me feel lost and bewildered.

Even though I was raised in a Christian environment, attended church, and joined youth groups, something was lacking. My life had a gaping hole that nothing could fill. Religion seemed abstract, prayers were customary, and God looked distant and impersonal. I was searching for something, but I had no idea where to find it.

I was reborn at the age of 8. After school, I would rush home and head straight to the living room, eager to look at the pictures in the Bible. The image of Jesus wrestling Jacob always mesmerized me. Determined to understand more, I taught myself to read the big words. I soon noticed that whenever I asked God questions in my mind, He would answer, and I would receive what I needed.

God became my family and my friend. We developed a very close relationship that felt even stronger than the bond of a brother. I vividly remember the moment I repeated the sinner's prayer while watching a Christian program. That prayer marked the beginning of my journey with God, and from that day forward, He has been a constant, guiding presence in my life.

Our church held a summer youth camp in the country. We took a few days off to pray, talk, and contemplate. I went because I thought the scenery and spiritual reflection would help me figure things out. It was a surprise that this retreat would improve my life.

One evening, the church service was exciting. The worship team sang songs about not giving up, faith, and the Holy Spirit. As I sang, I was moved by the lyrics and wanted to dedicate my heart to God for the first time.

When the service leader called for prayer requests, I wasn't sure what to do. Despite being afraid and confused, I reached the front. One leader put his hand on my shoulder and prayed as I closed my eyes. I felt vulnerable and excited.

I experienced an overwhelming sense of love at that moment as an intense emotion coursed through my heart and body. Tears covered my cheeks, but not because I was upset; I was thrilled to be loved and understood. My loneliness and confusion vanished, leaving me with unbelievable serenity and joy.

That was my first Holy Spirit experience. It was like a veil was lifted, and I could see and sense God's presence. I felt the Holy Spirit in every aspect of my life, not just as a notion. That day transformed my relationship with God. A discussion replaced the ritual. Worship became more than a habit—it showed affection. My relationship with Jesus Christ became alive.

Did I get all my questions answered? Did my life improve following this meeting? Absolutely not. I gained confidence and power I could utilize anytime and anywhere. I had the

Holy Spirit as my guidance, support, and companion. He taught, chastised, applauded, and gave me the strength to live my faith in ways I never imagined possible.

I pray this narrative brings the Holy Spirit into your heart. The Holy Spirit is eager to meet you wherever you are in your spiritual journey, whether you have questions or wish to become closer to God. He is gentle, compassionate, and patient and wants to empower you.

After reading this book, you can begin your spiritual journey. In the following pages, I will share additional stories, insights, and tips to strengthen your relationship with Him. We will explore the freedom, joy, and purpose of following the Holy Spirit and the amazing things that can happen. Let's start with hearts open to the Holy Spirit's love and power.

Chapter Overview and Roadmap

Understanding where we are going as we start this life-changing journey together is important. Each part of "LIFE WITH THE HOLY SPIRIT" is meant to build on the one before it, helping you fully understand and experience the Holy Spirit in your life. Each part will have the following:

Chapter 1: Understanding Your Salvation

In this first chapter, I will discuss salvation and how accepting Jesus improves your life. I will break down salvation into simple stages that everyone seeking God can follow. I will emphasize honesty and self-confidence to demonstrate how these characteristics can lead to a new life. I will discuss how remarkable it is that God forgives and forgets our mistakes using real-life instances. You will learn how to strengthen your faith via everyday behaviors and mindset adjustments. Inspiring stories of personal growth will demonstrate the power of salvation. Finally, we will discuss the sinner's prayer and how to say it with joy rather than fear. I will also explore how accepting Jesus unlocks the benefits of forgiveness.

Chapter 2: Getting to Know the Holy Spirit

Chapter 2 discusses the Holy Spirit, a crucial aspect of the Trinity that is sometimes overlooked, and describes His character. We will discuss how the Holy Spirit guides us in making minor decisions. Giving readers ways to detect the Holy Spirit will help them listen to His gentle instruction. Discuss how to form a lifelong relationship with the Holy Spirit, like making friends, and share examples of how different individuals experience Him. We will explain the significance of being baptized in the Holy Spirit and offer a brief prayer for people to reflect on how accepting Him may transform them.

Chapter 3: Growing Stronger in Your Faith

Renewing your intellect aids spiritual progress; I will illustrate its importance with daily examples in this chapter. I will discuss basic faith-building steps you can take right now in your busy modern life. I will address common questions and provide honest answers and support to those in need. Teaching good reading and comprehension abilities will make the Bible more useful. I will discuss applying scripture to modern issues. To emphasize the importance of community in spiritual growth, I will encourage readers to seek support from other believers and discuss the significance of choosing spiritual guidance and community wisely.

Chapter 4: Living Fully with the Holy Spirit

This chapter talks about recognizing the Holy Spirit's direction in small and big decisions you make every day. I will talk about a helpful way to use spiritual knowledge and common sense to make important choices with the help of the Holy Spirit. We will discuss ways to find your God-given interests and purpose and encourage you to look into your unique gifts. I will discuss how the Holy Spirit can transform relationships, including family, friendships, and romantic partnerships. We will also share the true stories of people who made significant changes by following the Holy Spirit's leadership. At the end of the chapter, I challenge readers to take a chance on faith and fully live their lives with the Holy Spirit.

Chapter 5: Understanding the Gifts of the Spirit

This chapter outlines the Holy Spirit's talents in simple words. It will cover self-reflection and feedback to discover your spiritual gifts, methods to cultivate and devote yourself to your spiritual gifts, and how assisting others can bring you a sense of fulfillment. Real-life stories of people who used their spiritual gifts to improve will be shown to demonstrate the significance of each gift and urge readers to value their own and other's gifts.

Chapter 6: Overcoming Challenges with the Holy Spirit

The Holy Spirit helps you overcome life's challenges. This chapter will discuss realistic solutions to peer pressure and temptation using the Holy Spirit. Our discussion on finding inner power during hard times will emphasize a close relationship with the Holy Spirit. We will use everyday examples to demonstrate how the Holy Spirit comforts and encourages us. We will discuss spiritual practices and living skills to become more robust via faith. Personal anecdotes of problem-solving with the help of the Holy Spirit will be a source of inspiration for you. There will also be a discussion on how faith may help you grow, how to recognize obstacles as spiritual opportunities, and how crucial it is to renew your faith daily and avoid lies.

Chapter 7: Sharing Your Faith with Others

We will discuss the benefits of sharing your religion with others. Tips on talking about Jesus without sounding aggressive or critical will be provided. You will learn how to use your life story to inspire others and make it a powerful witness. How can you be a good person in your community, and how may faith motivate you to act? We will discuss typical worries and challenges that make sharing faith difficult and provide hope and solutions. Talks will include creative and respectful ways to express your opinions at school, work, and social media. The emphasis will be on loving everyone, even people of various religions.

Chapter 8: Your Future with the Holy Spirit

This final chapter explores God's mystery and His fascinating plan for each person's existence. We will become practical strategists connected to the Holy Spirit and form lasting spiritual habits. I will discuss the concept of eternal vision to assist readers in understanding their faith journey. We will explore how finding and embracing your place in God's plan can encourage you to think about others. Sharing stories where you felt led by the Holy Spirit can uplift and inspire you. At the end of the chapter, the challenge is to live each day with purpose and cooperate with the Holy Spirit to make the future meaningful.

Conclusion: Your Journey Continues

Each chapter will be reviewed with crucial lessons at the end and illustrate how they fit together to paint a complete picture of living with the Holy Spirit. I will passionately support your next steps and acknowledge that spiritual progress is a lifelong journey with ups and downs. However, I assure you that you are never alone. I will pray for your

Holy Spirit filling at the end; I want you all to adopt this prayer as you grow in faith.

Prayer For Salvation and The Baptism of The Holy Spirit;

Heavenly Father, I come to you in the name of your son, Jesus Christ.

You said in your word that whosoever shall call upon the name of the Lord Jesus shall be saved.

Father, I'm calling on Jesus right now.

I believe he died on the cross for my sins, that he was raised from the dead on the third day, and that he's alive right now.

Holy Spirit, come into my heart and be my lord and guide.

To receive the infilling of the holy spirit, after repeating the salvation prayer: father god, I am your child.

I believe in my heart that Jesus was raised from the dead, and I confess to him as my Lord and Savior.

Chapter 1: Understanding Your Salvation

The term "salvation" signifies being saved and experiencing a life-changing event. In this new universe, you can forget your mistakes and make changes to improve your future. Imagine lugging a large rucksack full of regrets and mistakes. Jesus lifts that burden when you accept him. Walk freely without guilt or humiliation.

Being saved involves believing that Jesus Christ, the Son of God, came into the world, lived a faultless life, and died on the cross for our sins. Discovering that God loves us despite our flaws and sins is life-changing. This affection doesn't depend on our actions or skill; He is loving and merciful. Everything changes when you accept Jesus. You must connect with Him, not merely pray. Because of our intimate friendship, you can talk to Him about everything. Jesus will be your buddy, aid, and savior. He consoles and advises you in good and terrible situations.

When I accepted Jesus as my savior, I felt calm like never before, like my heart was lit up. This light clarified and enriched my life; I suddenly had a cause to live, not just survive. I felt welcome and valuable because I was adored, and forgiveness is one of the best parts of salvation. We make errors, but God forgives us. The Bible states He forgets and throws our sins into the sea. If you follow Jesus, your history doesn't define you because your start is fresh.

How would you feel if someone wiped the whiteboard clean after you made mistakes? Would you feel better? Would you be thankful? Christ does that for us. He overlooks our blunders and starts afresh. You forgive us because you trust us, not because we deserve it.

You must strengthen your faith daily to live in grace because prayer is a powerful means of reaching God. In this lecture, say what you believe, feel, and hope. The Bible explains God's will for your life. It's like a roadmap for life's challenges.

Worship is also vital as it goes beyond church songs—it's a lifestyle. Living is serving God in all you do; you can worship God in school, work, or home, using your actions and thoughts. Worship and daily life can bring you closer to God.

Many people start their journey of forgiveness with the simple yet powerful prayer of the sinner. This prayer acknowledges your need for Jesus and invites Him in. The sinner's prayer can be cheerful and sincere:

"Father in heaven, I pray to You in the name of Your Son, Jesus Christ. According to my relationship with Jesus Christ, he died on the cross for my sins and rose again. Forgive me for my mistakes. Be my Lord and Savior in my heart. You saved me and gave me a fresh life. Amen."

Accepting Jesus will change your life forever; Christ will change you. Your past sins and reputation no longer define you; God loves and cares about you. This new personality empowers you to live confidently and meaningfully.

There will be challenges and questions, but you are never alone. In the next chapter, we'll discuss your Holy Spirit. Be guided and strengthened by him. Open your heart to forgiveness and let Jesus' love alter your life.

Steps to Salvation

Understanding salvation can sometimes feel overwhelming, but it doesn't have to be. Here are straightforward steps to guide you through the process, breaking it down into easy-to-follow actions for anyone seeking God.

1. Acknowledge Your Need for Salvation: The first step is recognizing that you need salvation. This means understanding that we all have sinned and fallen short of God's glory (Romans 3:23). It's about admitting that you cannot achieve righteousness on your own and need God's help.

2. Believe in Jesus Christ: Salvation comes through believing that Jesus Christ is the Son of God, who died for your sins and rose again. This belief is more than acknowledging His existence; it's trusting in Him for your salvation. John 3:16 beautifully sums this up: "For God so loved the world that he gave his one and only Son, that whoever believes in him shall not perish but have eternal life."

3. Confess Your Sins: Confession is about being honest with God about your sins. It's not just about listing them but expressing genuine remorse and a desire to turn away. 1 John 1:9 assures us, "If we confess our sins, he is faithful and just and will forgive us and purify us from all unrighteousness."

4. Repentance: Repentance means a change of heart and mind, turning away from sin and toward God. It's an active decision to follow God's ways. Acts 3:19 says, "Repent, then, and turn to God, so that your sins may be wiped out, that times of refreshing may come from the Lord."

5. Accept Jesus as Your Savior: This step involves inviting Jesus to your life as your Lord and Savior. It's a personal commitment to follow Him and let Him lead your life. This can be done through the sinner's prayer, where you openly declare your faith and acceptance of Jesus Christ.

6. Receive the Holy Spirit: Upon accepting Jesus, you receive the Holy Spirit, who dwells within you, guiding and empowering you. The Holy Spirit helps you understand God's word, convicts you of sin, and equips you for righteous living. Acts 2:38 encourages us, "Repent and be baptized, every one of you, in the name of Jesus Christ for the forgiveness of your sins. And you will receive the gift of the Holy Spirit."

7. Commit to a New Life: Salvation is the beginning of a new life in Christ. This means committing to growing in your faith through regular prayer, reading the Bible, and joining a community of believers. It involves surrendering to God's will and allowing Him to transform your life.

8. Live Out Your Faith: Finally, living out your faith means demonstrating the change in your life through your actions. It's about being a light in the world, showing love, kindness, and the fruits of the Spirit (Galatians 5:22-23). It's about sharing the good news of Jesus with others and living a life that honors God.

Power Of Honest Confession and Heartfelt Belief

Confession and belief are not just rituals or formalities; they are potent acts that can potentially transform your life in profound ways. When you come before God with an honest confession and a heartfelt belief, you open the door to a new life filled with hope, peace, and purpose. The Bible tells us in 1 John 1:9, "If we confess our sins, he is faithful and just and will forgive us our sins and purify us from all unrighteousness." This promise assures us that no matter what we have done, God is ready to forgive us when we come to Him with a repentant heart.

Confession is powerful because it breaks the guilt and shame that often hold us back. When we hide our sins, they fester and grow, creating a barrier between us and God. But when we confess them, we bring them into the light, allowing God's grace to wash over and cleanse us. Bringing our sins to light frees us from their power and will enable us to experience God's forgiveness and healing.

Heartfelt belief is the other side of the coin. It's about genuinely trusting in Jesus Christ as your Lord and Savior. This belief goes beyond mere intellectual acknowledgment;

it involves trusting and trusting in Him. Romans 10:9 says, "If you declare with your mouth, 'Jesus is Lord,' and believe in your heart that God raised him from the dead, you will be saved." This verse emphasizes the importance of both confession and belief in salvation.

Believing in Jesus means trusting His sacrifice on the cross was sufficient to pay the penalty for your sins. It means accepting that His resurrection gives you the promise of new life, both now and for eternity. This belief is not just a one-time event; it's a continuous, growing trust in Jesus that shapes your thoughts, actions, and attitudes.

Combining honest confession with heartfelt belief opens the door to a new life in Christ. Several key changes mark this new life:

1. Peace with God: Confession and belief restore your relationship with God, giving you peace that surpasses understanding. This peace comes from knowing that your sins are forgiven and your Creator loves you unconditionally.

2. Freedom from Guilt and Shame: Honest confession releases you from guilt and shame. When you lay your sins at the feet of Jesus, He takes them away, allowing you to live freely and joyfully

3. New Identity: In Christ, you become a new creation. Your past no longer defines you; instead, your identity is rooted in God's love and grace. 2 Corinthians 5:17 declares, "Therefore, if anyone is in Christ, the new creation has come: The old has gone, the new is here!"

4. Purpose and Direction: Believing in Jesus gives your life purpose and direction. You no longer wander; you have a clear sense of purpose, guided by God's will for your life. This purpose involves growing in your faith, serving others, and sharing the love of Christ with the world.

5. Empowerment by the Holy Spirit: When you confess and believe, you receive the Holy Spirit, who empowers you to live a godly life. The Holy Spirit guides you, convicts you of sin, and equips you with spiritual gifts to serve others and glorify God.

6. Hope for the Future: In Christ, you have a living hope that sustains you through life's challenges. This hope is rooted in the promise of eternal life and the assurance that God is with you every step of the way.

A sincere apology and a strong belief are powerful because they help you live the life God wants. They let you feel how much He loves you, how much kindness He gives you, and how happy He is to be with you. Remember that confession and belief are things you always do as you walk this path of faith. Always tell God about your problems and sins, and always say that you trust Jesus. By doing this, you will get closer to Him and live the whole life He offers.

God's power to forgive and forget our mistakes is truly unique and different from anything we experience with other people. It can be difficult to fully comprehend this kindness because it contradicts our usual observations. People who have hurt others often remember what they did, even after they have been forgiven. On the other hand, God works on a different level. His forgiveness isn't just a hesitant pardon; it erases all our sins from His mind and our history.

Imagine you have a whiteboard covered in all your mistakes, regrets, and wrongdoings. Every lie, every act of unkindness, every moment of weakness is there for all to see. Now, picture someone coming with a cloth and wiping that whiteboard clean, leaving no trace of the past marks. This is what God does with our sins. When we go to Him in confession and belief, He wipes our slate clean. The Bible says in Isaiah 1:18, "Though your sins are like scarlet, they shall be as white as snow; though they are red as crimson, they shall be like wool." This illustrates the thoroughness of God's forgiveness.

To make this more relatable, think about a time when you hurt a close friend. You might have apologized, and your friend might have said they forgive you, but a lingering memory of the incident often affects your relationship. Now, contrast this with God's forgiveness. He doesn't hold grudges or keep a record of wrongs. Psalm 103:12 tells us, "As far as the east is from the west, so far has he removed our transgressions from us." This means that once God forgives, He completely separates us from our sins. They are no longer part of our identity or our relationship with Him.

Consider the story of the Prodigal Son in Luke 15:11-32. The younger son demands his inheritance early, squanders it in reckless living, and ends up destitute. When he decides to return home, he expects to be treated as a servant, not a son. But his father sees him from afar, runs to him, embraces him, and throws a lavish party to celebrate his return. The father doesn't dwell on the son's past mistakes. Instead, he celebrates his return with complete joy and restoration. This parable illustrates God's readiness to forgive and restore us, no matter how far we have strayed.

Another example can be seen in the life of the Apostle Peter. Peter denied Jesus three times during the hours leading up to the crucifixion. This was a significant betrayal, and Peter was deeply ashamed of his actions. After Jesus' resurrection, He meets Peter and asks him three times if he loves Him, allowing Peter to reaffirm his love and commitment. Jesus doesn't bring up Peter's denials to shame him; instead, He focuses on restoring their relationship and commissioning Peter for future service. This shows how God forgives and reinstates us to a place of honor and purpose, regardless of our past.

God's forgiveness is also evident in how He treats us after we confess our sins. He doesn't keep bringing up our past mistakes to punish or shame us. Instead, He encourages us to move forward in freedom. Micah 7:19 says, "You will again have compassion on us; you will tread our sins underfoot and hurl all our iniquities into the depths of the sea." This vivid imagery helps us understand that God's forgiveness is final and complete. Our sins are not just out of sight but utterly removed and dealt with.

This incredible gift of forgiveness is something that we can lean on every day. Whenever we fall short, we can confidently approach God, knowing He will forgive us and forget our sins. This isn't a license to live recklessly but an invitation to live freely, secure in the knowledge that God's love and grace cover us. As we experience this forgiveness, we are also called to extend it to others, reflecting God's grace in our relationships.

Building a solid foundation for your faith is crucial for sustaining a meaningful and fulfilling spiritual life. This foundation is built through daily habits and mindset shifts that help you stay connected to God and grow in your relationship with Him. Here are some practical ways to strengthen your faith:

1. **Pray every day:** Prayer is a solid way to talk to God. It doesn't need to be long or hard to understand. Say a simple prayer of thanks to God in Jesus' name for all the good things in your life, and ask Him to lead you. Keep talking to God throughout the day, telling him your thoughts, worries, and joys. Before bed, think about the day and ask God to be with you. Being consistent with your prayers will help you get closer to God.

2. **Read and study the Bible**: The Bible is God's word and one of the most important ways to learn about His will and promises. Every day, set aside time to read the Bible and think about what it says. One sentence or chapter a day is an excellent place to start. You might want to use a Bible reading plan to help you learn. Think about what you read and ask God to show you how to use it in your own life. Learning about the Bible makes you smarter and your faith stronger.

3. Worship: Worship isn't just for Sunday events; you do it daily. You can praise God by singing, playing music, or just telling Him how much you love and appreciate Him. Worship takes your mind off of your worries and emphasizes how great and loving God is. Having it with Him brings you peace and refreshes your spirit. Every day, worship God, whether it's through music, prayer, or just quiet thoughts.

4. Community and Fellowship: Your spiritual growth needs to be part of a group of Christians. Joining a church, small group, or Bible study in your area can help you meet new people, share your stories, and help each other. Being with other Christians gives you support, holds you accountable, and gives you chances to help. It helps you remember that you are not the only one on your religious journey.

5. Service and Giving: Showing your faith by helping others and giving freely are two ways you can do this. Find ways to help people who need it, whether by working, doing nice things for them, or giving them money. Giving to others is a way to follow Jesus' lessons and become more compassionate and humble. It makes you happy and satisfied to know you are making a difference for the better.

6. Mindset Shifts: Developing a mindset that fits your faith is essential. Believe that God has a good plan for your life, and think positively. When problems come up, don't give in to fear or doubt. Instead, remember God's promises and how faithful He is. Regularly thanking God for His gifts is an excellent way to show gratitude. Being thankful and cheerful helps you see God's hand in everything and builds trust in Him.

7. Learn Bible lines by heart: This will help you remember God's word, especially when needed. Choose the lines that resonate with you, and recite them daily until you internalize them. Reading the Bible can help you feel better, give you direction, and strengthen you. It also makes it easier to share God's word with others.

8. Writing in a journal: Writing down your spiritual journey can be beneficial. Write down your thoughts, prayers, and memories. Write down the answers to your questions and the new ideas you get from studying the Bible. Keep a journal to see how you've changed, find trends, and see how God has worked in your life. There's also a record of your faith journey that you can use to get more strength.

9. Regular Self-Examination and Reflection: Think about your spiritual life regularly. Look at your growth, your habits, and your bond with God. Ask yourself if there are things you could do better or habits you should change. If you look at yourself, you can stay on track and be intentional about your religious journey.

10. Looking for Help and Advice: Find a spiritual guide or instructor to help you with your faith. This person can give you advice, hold you accountable, and help. They can help you deal with problems, answer your questions, and provide you with advice based on what they've seen and done. Having a mentor keeps you steady and on track with your spiritual growth.

Changing these habits and ways of thinking daily builds a strong foundation for your faith. This base helps you stay close to God, grow closer to Him, and live out your faith profoundly. Building a good foundation takes time and effort, but the benefits are enormous. It helps you connect better with God and live a life full of His love, peace, and purpose.

Stories from real people whose lives have been changed by accepting Jesus show how mighty salvation can be and how its ideas can come to life. Here are some moving stories that show what a fantastic trip it is from being broken to being whole through Christ.

From Despair to Hope

As a child, Sarah didn't have much love in her home. Her parents fought all the time, and she often felt like no one saw or loved her. As she turned thirteen, Sarah looked for approval and acceptance in bad relationships and dangerous actions. No matter what she did, she always felt like her heart was missing something.

Sarah went to a nearby park one night after a nasty fight with her parents because she felt completely lost. She saw an older woman named Mary reading the Bible in silence. Mary noticed that Sarah was upset, so she started a quiet talk and told Sarah she had found hope in Jesus after a complicated past. Sarah agreed to attend church with Mary the following Sunday because she was interested in her peace and joy.

Sarah was moved by the word of God's love and the community she felt at church. The preacher talked about what Jesus did and how it gives people who believe a new start. Sarah's heart began to move, and with tears in her eyes that day, she made Jesus her Savior.

Sarah's life changed after that. She found a group of people who could help her at church and started going to a youth group. Through praying and reading the Bible, Sarah learned to believe that God loved her instead of feeling like she wasn't worth anything. The knowledge that her Heavenly Father loved and cared for her filled the hole in her heart. Sarah is now a youth leader and helps other kids find hope and meaning in Christ.

Getting Clean from Drugs

John's life was getting worse because he was hooked on drugs. He lost his job, relationships, and health because of something that started as a way for him to deal with stress and group pressure. He felt stuck and hopeless and thought he could never be saved.

John hit rock bottom one night after a terrible accident that sent him to the hospital. He knew he couldn't keep living this way while he was lying in the hospital bed. A chaplain went to see him and told him the story of the Prodigal Son to calm him. The priest told John that nobody could hurt him and that God would always love and forgive him.

John was desperate to make a change, so after he got out of jail, he chose to go to a Christian rehab center. There, he learned about giving up his life for Jesus. John began to understand how much God loved him through daily Bible study, prayer, and the help of other Christians. He admitted his mistakes and accepted Jesus as his Savior. After that, he felt free and at peace like never before.

John's life didn't change immediately, but he beat his problem with hard work and faith. Building his new life on God's love, he now shares his story with others dealing with addiction, giving them hope and encouragement through his journey of redemption.

Healing from Emotional Hurts

Emily had always felt very bad about herself and rejected. As a child in a broken home, she took on board the mean things people said and did, which made her very depressed and anxious. Emily did well in school and her career, but she still felt like she wasn't good enough to be loved and accepted.

A friend asked Emily to a church-hosted retreat for women. Emily was unsure at first, but she chose to go because she wanted a break from her daily problems. The speakers at the retreat talked about how God's love can heal and how important it is to see oneself through His eyes. A session deeply touched Emily on forgiving and letting go of hurts from the past.

Emily opened her heart to God in a quiet moment of thought. She told Him how inadequate she felt and asked Him to help her. At that moment, she felt God's love and presence all around her, reassuring her that He loved her as His daughter. Emily had a deep sense of acceptance and peace that she had never had before.

When Emily returned home, she continued to grow in her faith by praying, studying the Bible, and attending church every week. She got better emotionally and learned to see herself the way God did: as valuable, loved, and deserving. Emily is now a counselor who helps people find healing and peace through Christ's love.

From Anger to Forgiveness

Mike was angry with his father because he had left the family when he was young. His anger affected every part of his life, from work to personal relationships. Even though Mike had done well, he was sad and angry because he couldn't get over how his father had hurt him.

Mike was asked to attend church service by a coworker. The sermon was about how powerful it is to forgive. The preacher told how Jesus forgave everyone on the cross, even those who had hurt Him. Mike was deeply moved and started to understand that staying angry made him feel worse.

Mike talked to the preacher after the service. The pastor told him to pray and ask God to help him forgive. It wasn't easy, but Mike slowly let go of his anger with the help of prayer and the people at his church. He tried to get along with his dad, which began the process of making things right.

It felt great for Mike to forgive his father. He felt free and at peace like he had never felt before. It also changed how he interacted with others, which helped him love more deeply and live more happily. Mike now tells others about his path of forgiveness and encourages them to experience how God's grace can change their lives.

These true stories of change show what a vast difference it makes when you accept Jesus into your life. Even if you've done bad things in the past, God's love, forgiveness, and grace can heal you, make things right, and give you a fresh start. Salvation isn't just an idea; it's an authentic experience that gives people hope, happiness, and a reason to live.

A big part of getting forgiven is saying the "sinner's prayer." This is a simple but robust way to show that you trust Jesus as your Lord and Savior. For many, this prayer is the beginning of a new life. Know how important this experience is and go into it with joy instead of fear or nervousness. It will be even more valuable and powerful.

Saying the sinner's prayer is significant because it shows that you believe in Jesus Christ. Someone must genuinely feel sorry for their sins and ask Jesus to take over their life to do this. When you say this prayer, you promise to give up sin and follow the Holy Spirit instead. Romans 10:9 says: "You will be saved if you say with your mouth, 'Jesus is Lord,' and believe in your heart that God raised him from the dead." This is an essential thing you can do to get closer to God.

Going into the sinner's prayer with joy instead of fear or nervousness can change your life. Here's how to happily accept this prayer:

1. Understanding God's Love:

Recognize that God's invitation to salvation is motivated by His deep and unconditional love for you. John 3:16 reminds us, "For God so loved the world that he gave his one and only Son, that whoever believes in him shall not perish but have eternal life." Understanding that you are loved by God just as you are can replace fear with joy. God is not looking for perfection; He is looking for a willing heart.

2. Focusing on the Positive Transformation:

The sinner's prayer is the gateway to a new life filled with hope, peace, and purpose. It's about leaving your past behind and stepping into a bright future with God. Think about the positive changes that will come with this decision: the peace of mind, the joy of being forgiven, and the strength to overcome challenges. This forward-looking perspective can fill your heart with joy and anticipation.

3. Relishing the Moment of Surrender:

Surrendering your life to Jesus through the sinner's prayer is an act of liberation. It's about letting go of guilt, shame, and sin and allowing God to control. This surrender is not a loss but a gain. Jesus said in Matthew 11:28, "Come to me, all you who are weary and burdened, and I will give you rest." Embrace the relief and freedom from placing your life in God's hands.

4. Celebrating with Others:

Share this moment with a trusted friend, family member, or pastor if possible. Having someone pray with you or be present can support and amplify this significant step's joy. Many churches celebrate new believers and their decision to follow Christ, making the experience even more joyous. Knowing you are joining a family of believers who will support and encourage you can bring great comfort and happiness.

5. Personalizing the Prayer:

While there are many versions of the sinner's prayer, making it personal can enhance its significance. Speak from your heart, using words that express your unique journey and feelings. This personal touch can make the prayer feel more genuine and heartfelt, reducing any nervousness you might feel. Remember, God knows your heart and values your sincerity over eloquence.

A sinner's prayer that you can personalize:

"Heavenly Father, I come to You in the name of Your Son, Jesus Christ. I believe He died on the cross for my sins and rose from the dead. I ask You to forgive me for all my sins. Jesus, come into my heart and be my Lord and Savior. Thank You for saving me and giving me a new life. Help me to follow You all the days of my life. Amen."

Approach this prayer with a spirit of joy, knowing it is the beginning of a beautiful journey with God. There is no need to fear or feel nervous because God's arms are wide open, ready to welcome you into His family. Embrace the joy of salvation, the peace of forgiveness, and the excitement of a new life in Christ. This is a moment to celebrate and mark the start of a beautiful relationship with Jesus that will transform your life forever.

Accepting Jesus as your Savior is a life-altering decision that brings immediate benefits, transforming your heart, mind, and soul. These benefits are not just promises for the future; they begin when you accept Christ into your life, marking the start of a profound and joyous journey.

Firstly, you experience immediate forgiveness of sins. The Bible assures us that "If we confess our sins, he is faithful and just to forgive us our sins and to cleanse us from all unrighteousness" (1 John 1:9). This means that the moment you accept Jesus, all your past sins are forgiven, and you are washed clean. The burden of guilt and shame is lifted, giving you a fresh start and a clear conscience.

Secondly, you receive the gift of the Holy Spirit. Acts 2:38 states, "Repent and be baptized, every one of you, in the name of Jesus Christ for the forgiveness of your sins. And you will receive the gift of the Holy Spirit." The Holy Spirit begins to dwell within you, guiding, comforting, and empowering you to live a life that honors God. This immediate presence of the Holy Spirit brings a sense of peace, assurance, and divine companionship.

Another immediate benefit is the restoration of your relationship with God. Sin separates us from God, but accepting Jesus bridges that gap. Romans 5:1 explains, "Therefore since we have been justified through faith, we have peace with God through our Lord Jesus Christ." This peace with God means you are no longer estranged from Him; instead, you are welcomed into His family as a beloved child. This restored relationship brings a profound sense of belonging and purpose.

You also gain a new identity in Christ. 2 Corinthians 5:17 declares, "Therefore, if anyone is in Christ, the new creation has come: The old has gone, the new is here!" From the moment you accept Jesus, you are no longer defined by your past mistakes or the world's labels. You are a new creation with a new identity rooted in God's love and grace. This new identity empowers you to live confidently and boldly, knowing that your Creator values and cherishes you.

Furthermore, you are given eternal life. John 3:16 promises, "For God so loved the world that he gave his one and only Son, that whoever believes in him shall not perish but have eternal life." This eternal life begins now and continues forever. It gives you hope and assurance that your future is secure, no matter what challenges you face.

Lastly, you become part of a global family of believers. Ephesians 2:19 says, "Consequently, you are no longer foreigners and strangers, but fellow citizens with God's people and also members of his household." This means you are now part of a community that spans the globe, offering support, encouragement, and fellowship. This sense of community can be incredibly uplifting, providing you with a network of friends and mentors who share your faith journey.

These immediate benefits of salvation – forgiveness, the Holy Spirit, restored relationship with God, new identity, eternal life, and community – are just the beginning. They lay the foundation for a life of growth, transformation, and purpose. Embrace these gifts with joy and gratitude, knowing they are a testament to God's incredible love for you. As you continue your journey, remember that these blessings are not just for today but the starting point of a lifelong adventure with Jesus, filled with His presence, guidance, and unending love.

With this foundation laid, we will continue exploring and deepening our understanding of living with the Holy Spirit in the following chapters. Embrace your new life with confidence, knowing that God is with you every step of the way.

Knowing about your salvation

This works for everybody; there is no need to be scared or nervous when reciting the sinner's prayer to unbelievers. You should be overjoyed because this is the single best thing you can do for yourself. When you become saved, you can start receiving all the benefits of salvation. Your benefits begin as soon as you are saved. You now have the holy spirit inside of you. Through his word, you will understand what's happening in your spirit.

Chapter 2: Getting to Know the Holy Spirit

The Holy Spirit, often referred to as the "Spirit of God," is an integral yet sometimes overlooked member of the Holy Trinity. Along with God the Father and Jesus Christ the Son, the Holy Spirit is an important and special part of Christians' lives and the story of Christianity as a whole. It is important to know and understand the Holy Spirit's presence, work, and nature in order to understand our faith fully.

From the very beginning of creation, the Holy Spirit has been actively involved. In Genesis 1:2, we read, "Now the earth was formless and empty, darkness was over the surface of the deep, and the Spirit of God was hovering over the waters." This imagery sets the stage for the Holy Spirit's creative and sustaining power. The Spirit's presence is not just a New Testament revelation but is woven throughout the entire biblical narrative, demonstrating His eternal nature and divine authority.

One of the Holy Spirit's primary roles is to act as a Comforter and Counselor. In John 14:16-17, Jesus promises His disciples, "And I will ask the Father, and He will give you another advocate to help you and be with you forever— the Spirit of truth. The world cannot accept Him because it neither sees Him nor knows Him. But you know Him, for He lives with you and will be in you." Here, Jesus assures His followers that the Holy Spirit will be their eternal companion, providing guidance, comfort, and support in His physical absence. This comforting presence is a hallmark of the Holy Spirit's personality, offering believers a sense of peace and assurance amidst life's challenges.

The Holy Spirit also plays a critical role in the process of sanctification, which is the transformative journey of becoming more like Christ. According to 2 Corinthians 3:18, "And we all, who with unveiled faces contemplate the Lord's glory, are being transformed into His image with ever-increasing glory, which comes from the Lord, who is the Spirit." The Holy Spirit works within us, gradually molding our character and actions to reflect the nature of Jesus. This transformation is a continuous process, illustrating the Spirit's patience and dedication to our spiritual growth.

Another vital aspect of the Holy Spirit's work is His role in imparting spiritual gifts. These gifts, described in 1 Corinthians 12:4-11, are given to believers to build up the body of Christ and to serve others effectively. The passage states, "There are different kinds of gifts, but the same Spirit distributes them. There are different kinds of service, but the same Lord. There are different kinds of work, but in all of them and in everyone, it is the same God." The diversity of these gifts—from wisdom and knowledge to healing and prophecy—demonstrates the Holy Spirit's dynamic and multifaceted nature. He empowers believers uniquely, enabling us to fulfill our specific callings within the church and the world.

The Holy Spirit is also known for His role in conviction. In John 16:8, Jesus explains, "When He comes, He will prove the world to be in the wrong about sin and righteousness and judgment." This convicting work is essential for leading people to repentance and faith in Jesus Christ. The Spirit illuminates the truth of the gospel, revealing our need for a Savior and guiding us toward a life of holiness. This aspect of the Holy Spirit's personality highlights His commitment to truth and justice, ensuring that we live in alignment with God's will.

The Holy Spirit is our guide into all truth. Jesus tells His disciples in John 16:13, "But when He, the Spirit of truth, comes, He will guide you into all the truth. He will not speak on His own; He will speak only what He hears, and He will tell you what is yet to come." The Holy Spirit enlightens our understanding of Scripture, helping us to grasp the deeper meanings and applications of God's Word. This guidance is crucial for our spiritual discernment and growth, enabling us to navigate the complexities of life with divine wisdom.

The personality of the Holy Spirit is further evidenced by His ability to intercede for us. Romans 8:26-27 states, "In the same way, the Spirit helps us in our weakness. We do not know what we ought to pray for, but the Spirit Himself intercedes for us through wordless groans. And He who searches our hearts knows the mind of the Spirit because the Spirit intercedes for God's people in accordance with the will of God." In our moments of uncertainty and weakness, the Holy Spirit steps in, praying on our behalf and aligning our requests with God's perfect will. This intercessory role underscores the Spirit's deep empathy and intimate knowledge of our hearts.

How the Holy Spirit Actively Works in Our Everyday Lives

The Holy Spirit's involvement in our lives is both profound and intimate, influencing everything from our smallest decisions to the most significant moments. Understanding how the Holy Spirit works daily can deepen our relationship with Him and enhance our spiritual journey.

Firstly, the Holy Spirit acts as our guide, offering subtle promptings and nudges that steer us in the right direction. These promptings can come in various forms, such as a sudden thought, a feeling of peace, or a sense of urgency. For example, you might feel a gentle urge to call a friend who has been on your mind, only to discover they needed encouragement at that moment. These small promptings are the Holy Spirit's way of guiding us to be the hands and feet of Jesus, showing love and care to those around us.

In our everyday decisions, the Holy Spirit provides wisdom and discernment. James 1:5 assures us, "If any of you lacks wisdom, you should ask God, who gives generously to all without finding fault, and it will be given to you." When faced with choices, whether minor or significant, we can seek the Holy Spirit's guidance to make decisions that align with God's will. This divine wisdom helps us navigate our relationships, career paths, and personal challenges, ensuring that our choices reflect God's character and purposes.

The Holy Spirit also plays a vital role in our spiritual growth by convicting us of sin and leading us to repentance. John 16:8 says, "When He comes, He will prove the world to be wrong about sin, righteousness, and judgment." This conviction is not about condemnation but about gently revealing areas in our lives that need correction. Through this process, the Holy Spirit helps us grow in holiness, transforming our character to become more like Christ. This continuous refinement is crucial for our spiritual maturity.

The Holy Spirit empowers us to live out our faith boldly. Acts 1:8 declares, "But you will receive power when the Holy Spirit comes on you, and you will be my witnesses in Jerusalem, and in all Judea and Samaria, and to the ends of the earth." This empowerment enables us to overcome fear, share the gospel, and serve others with courage and conviction. Whether it's standing up for justice, speaking truth in love, or extending compassion to the needy, the Holy Spirit equips us to make a meaningful impact in the world.

In times of difficulty and uncertainty, the Holy Spirit offers comfort and peace. Jesus promised in John 14:26-27, "But the Advocate, the Holy Spirit, whom the Father will send in my name, will teach you all things and will remind you of everything I have said to you. Peace I leave with you; my peace I give you." When we face trials, the Holy Spirit reassures us of God's presence and love, providing a peace that transcends our understanding. This inner peace helps us endure hardships with hope and resilience.

The Holy Spirit also cultivates the fruit of the Spirit within us, as outlined in Galatians 5:22-23: "But the fruit of the Spirit is love, joy, peace, forbearance, kindness, goodness, faithfulness, gentleness and self-control." These qualities reflect the Holy Spirit's work in our lives, transforming our behavior and attitudes. As we yield to the Spirit, these attributes become more evident, enhancing our relationships and testimony.

Practical Ways to Recognize the Holy Spirit's Presence

Recognizing the Holy Spirit's presence and tuning into His gentle guidance is essential to a vibrant Christian life. The Holy Spirit speaks to us in various ways, and developing sensitivity to His voice can enhance our spiritual journey and decision-making processes.

One of the most effective ways to tune into the Holy Spirit is through regular prayer and meditation. Prayer opens a line of communication with God, allowing us to speak and listen. During these times, the Holy Spirit can impress thoughts, ideas, or scriptures upon our hearts. Setting aside quiet moments for meditation helps us clear our minds of distractions and focus on God's voice. Practicing stillness and attentiveness during prayer can help us become more aware of the Holy Spirit's subtle promptings.

The Holy Spirit often speaks through God's Word. Engaging in daily Bible reading allows the Holy Spirit to illuminate scriptures, providing insight and direction for our lives. Hebrews 4:12 describes the Word of God as "alive and active," and the Holy Spirit brings this living Word to life in our hearts. As we read, we should ask the Holy Spirit to guide our understanding and apply biblical truths to our circumstances. Keeping a journal to record insights and reflections can help us track how the Holy Spirit speaks to us through scripture.

A sense of inner peace often accompanies the Holy Spirit's guidance. Colossians 3:15 encourages us to "let the peace of Christ rule in your hearts." We can seek the Holy Spirit's direction by evaluating our sense of peace when making decisions. The Holy Spirit may affirm that decision if a particular choice brings deep, abiding peace. Conversely, if we feel unrest or confusion, it could signal us to reconsider or seek further clarity. Cultivating sensitivity to this peace can help us discern the Holy Spirit's guidance.

The Holy Spirit can use circumstances to direct us. Doors opening or closing, unexpected opportunities, and timely interventions can all be ways the Holy Spirit guides us. Paying attention to these signs requires spiritual discernment. We should prayerfully consider the circumstances in our lives and ask the Holy Spirit for wisdom to interpret them. Reflecting on how events align with God's Word and our prayers can provide valuable insights into the Holy Spirit's leading.

The Holy Spirit often speaks through the wisdom and advice of mature believers. Seeking counsel from trusted

Christian friends, mentors, or church leaders can help us discern the Holy Spirit's guidance. These individuals can offer perspectives and insights that we might not have considered, and their confirmation can affirm the Holy Spirit's leadership in our lives.

Sometimes, the Holy Spirit communicates by repeating messages through different sources. It may be the Holy Spirit trying to get your attention if you notice a particular scripture, theme, or advice recurring in your life—from sermons, books, conversations, or even songs. Paying attention to these repeated messages and prayerfully considering their significance can help us recognize the Holy Spirit's direction.

Being obedient to the Holy Spirit's promptings, even in small matters, sharpens our ability to hear His voice. Luke 16:10 says, "Whoever can be trusted with very little can also be trusted with much." We become more attuned to His voice when we respond to the Holy Spirit's guidance in everyday situations. Obedience builds a habit of responsiveness, making it easier to recognize and follow His leading in more significant decisions.

Reflecting on past experiences where you felt the Holy Spirit's guidance can help you recognize His presence in the future. Consider moments when you felt a strong sense of direction, peace, or conviction and how those experiences unfolded. By identifying patterns in how the Holy Spirit has worked in your life, you can become more attuned to His current and future guidance. Worship opens our hearts to the

Holy Spirit's presence. Singing, praising, and expressing gratitude to God invites the Holy Spirit to move in our hearts. Worship shifts our focus from our concerns to God's greatness, making us more receptive to His voice. Regularly engaging in prayer, both corporately and individually, creates an environment where the Holy Spirit's presence is more easily recognized.

Actively seeking the Holy Spirit's guidance shows our dependence on Him. James 1:5 encourages us to ask God for wisdom, including seeking the Holy Spirit's direction. Pray for the Holy Spirit's guidance in your decisions and daily life. Express your desire to be led by Him and your willingness to follow His promptings. By incorporating these practical steps into our daily lives, we can become more attuned to the Holy Spirit's presence and guidance. Recognizing the Holy Spirit's voice requires intentionality, sensitivity, and a heart open to His leading. As we grow in our relationship with the Holy Spirit, we will experience His transformative power and wisdom in every aspect of our lives.

Steps to develop a genuine, ongoing relationship with the Holy Spirit, much like building a friendship

Having a real, ongoing relationship with the Holy Spirit is a lot like having a close, important friendship. It takes time, effort, and being open to what is happening. To help you keep this divine friendship going, here are some steps:

Recognizing that the Holy Spirit is there is the first thing that you need to do to build a connection with Him.

Recognizing and greeting the Holy Spirit's presence in your life is like greeting a friend when they walk into the room. It sets the stage for a deeper relationship. Start your day by letting the Holy Spirit guide your thoughts and actions. A simple prayer like, "Holy Spirit, I welcome You into my day." Saying, "Guide me and fill me with Your presence," can change how you see Him and how you talk to Him.

It's important to spend time with the Holy Spirit. Like any other friendship, spending time together makes it stronger. Every day, make time to be with the Holy Spirit by yourself. One way to do this is to pray, meditate, or just be still and listen for His word. Making time to talk to the Holy Spirit a regular part of your life helps you get closer and more familiar with them.

It's important to talk to each other in every connection, and the Holy Spirit is no different. Talk to Him in an open and honest way. Share your happiness, worry, fear, and hopes. Don't forget that talking and listening go hand in hand; take the time to do both. The Holy Spirit talks to us in many ways, such as through the Bible, our own thoughts, and the advice of other people. Your relationship will improve if you pay attention and respond to what He says.

Having a thankful heart can help you connect with the Holy Spirit more deeply. Thanking Him for His help, comfort, and presence in your life on a regular basis will keep your mood positive and open. When you are grateful, you stop focusing on what is going wrong and start focusing on the good things and help the Holy Spirit gives you. This practice makes you more aware of how He is involved in your life and brings you closer to Him.

To have a friendship that lasts, you need to build trust. Believe that the Holy Spirit will lead you, even if you don't fully understand what He is telling you. "Trust in the Lord with all your heart and do not lean on your own understanding," says Proverbs 3:5–6. "Submit to Him in all your ways, and He will make your paths straight." When you trust the Holy Spirit, you depend on His knowledge and time, even if it goes against what you want or plan. Your trust in Him will grow as you see how reliable He is.

It's very important to listen to what the Holy Spirit says. You would show respect and loyalty to a friend by following their advice. Doing the same with the Holy Spirit shows that you are committed to the friendship. When you obey in both small and big situations, you form the habit of being responsive, which makes it easier to follow His direction in the future. This habit not only makes the Holy Spirit happy, but it also makes your life more in line with what God wants.

Worship and praise the Holy Spirit with other people. Because it makes you think and feel about how great and loving God is, worship is a solid way to connect with the Holy Spirit. When you sing, pray, and praise God, you ask the Holy Spirit to be with you and strengthen your connection. Worship takes your mind off of your problems and onto the greatness of God, which brings you closer to the Holy Spirit.

Be around other people who believe what you believe. A community of faith can help your relationship with the Holy Spirit grow, just like a supportive atmosphere can help friendships grow. Join a church or small group where you can learn from each other and grow as a person. A community can improve your spiritual journey and connection with the Holy Spirit by giving you support, holding you accountable, and sharing your knowledge.

Often think about your journey with the Holy Spirit. Take some time to remember the things that happened, the problems you faced, and how you grew. This will help you see the Holy Spirit's work in your life more clearly. Writing down your prayers, thoughts, and experiences with the Holy Spirit can help you feel better and gain new knowledge. This practice will help you see patterns, understand His guidance, and value the connection you are building with Him.

Don't give up, and keep trying. Getting close to the Holy Spirit takes time, just like getting close to any other person. There may be times when there is silence or when you feel far away, but it is important to keep going and be patient. Keep looking for, talking to, and listening to the Holy Spirit. Have faith that your efforts are creating a strong link that will last.

You can have a real, ongoing friendship with the Holy Spirit if you do these things. You can make your relationship with the Holy Spirit stronger and more personal by giving it time, trust, and being open. This is similar to how you grow bonds. Your bond with the Holy Spirit will grow stronger, and you will feel his presence and power in every part of your life.

Different people experience the Holy Spirit in different ways, which shows how personal our connection with God is. Different people have different experiences with the Holy Spirit, which shows how He can touch and change our lives in many ways:

1. How the Holy Spirit Can Help You Feel Better When You've Lost Someone:

Rebecca had a strong bond with her grandmother, who was a rock of faith in her family. As soon as Rebecca's grandmother died, she was filled with sadness and a deep sense of loss. As Rebecca sat in silent prayer at the funeral, she felt a great feeling of peace wash over her. It felt like the Holy Spirit was giving her a warm hug and reassuring her that her grandma was happy with God. Rebecca felt a lot better after this experience. It gave her hope and reassurance that she wasn't alone as she went through her loss.

2. The Holy Spirit as a Guide for Making Good God Choices:

David was in a tough spot in his job. There were two job offers in front of him: one would have paid him a lot more, but it wasn't really in line with his interests; the other would have allowed him to help people, but it would have paid less. David spent time praying to get help from the Holy Spirit because he couldn't make up his mind. During his quiet time one morning, David felt a strong urge to go after the job that fit his interests. He was calm and clear in a way that he had never felt before. He thought that following the Holy Spirit's lead was the direct cause of his work, which gave him meaning and fulfillment over time.

3. When the Holy Spirit inspires you to be creative:

Samantha often had trouble writing because she was a writer. When she was really stuck one day, she chose to take a break and pray and worship for a while. She had a sudden rush of creative thoughts after thinking about God's Word and letting the Holy Spirit fill her. It didn't take her long to get her notebook and start writing quickly. It was easy for her to write, and she finished her work in a record amount of time. Samantha knew that her sudden inspiration came from the Holy Spirit, who had opened up her imagination and given her new ways to express herself that she hadn't thought of before.

4. The Holy Spirit in Acts of Kindness:

Carlos was helping out at a local shelter for the poor when he saw a young woman sitting by herself and looking upset. He had a strong urge to go up to her and offer his help. Carlos followed her lead and sat down next to her to start a conversation. The young woman, whose name was Maria, told of her hard times. Carlos understood what she was saying and offered to pray with her. Through tears, Maria said she felt like a weight had been taken off her shoulders, and she had hope again that she hadn't had in a long time. It dawned on Carlos that the Holy Spirit had used him to show Maria kindness and comfort, giving her the help she needed at that time.

5. How the Holy Spirit Helps You Get Through Hard Times:

Emily had anxiety for years, and it often made her feel like she couldn't do anything. During a church meeting one evening, the pastor asked anyone who was having a hard time with anxiety to come forward and be prayed for. Emily was hesitant to go forward, but she needed help badly. Emily felt a deep sense of peace and calm surround her as the crowd prayed. In the weeks that followed, she realized that her anxiety levels dropped a lot. She started to feel freer and surer of herself in her daily life. Emily thought that the healing touch of the Holy Spirit was what had changed her and given her the strength to face her fears.

6. The Holy Spirit in Small Groups and Fellowship:

Michael talked about how hard it was for him to find meaning in his life at a small group Bible study. The group collected around him, put their hands on him, and prayed very hard. Michael felt a huge amount of love and support from his fellow Christians as they prayed. He felt the Holy Spirit telling him that he was important and valuable, which gave him a new sense of direction. Michael's faith grew stronger, and his relationship with his small group got stronger because of this experience. It showed him how important community and friendship are for experiencing the Holy Spirit.

7. How the Holy Spirit Helps Us Make Daily Choices:

Laura often prayed for help with the choices she made every day, from what to do at work to what to do in her personal life. She was thinking about whether to take on a hard job at work one day. She felt a soft but persistent push while she was praying, telling her to take on the task. Laura chose to follow this lead and took on the project. While going through the process, she gained knowledge and wisdom that were beyond her natural skills. To her credit, she finished the job well and was praised for it. Laura said that the Holy Spirit led her and gave her the knowledge she needed to deal with the problems.

8. The role of the Holy Spirit in changing relationships:

Tom had a rough time getting along with his brother, Mark. They had not talked in years, but during a lecture about forgiveness, Tom felt very strongly that we should engage ourselves. He felt the Holy Spirit telling him to talk to Mark and make peace. He called Mark, even though he was nervous, and to his surprise, Mark responded. They talked about how they felt, said they were sorry for hurting each other in the past, and decided to start over. It was clear that the Holy Spirit was at work in this reunion to heal and change relationships.

9. The Holy Spirit in Encouraging Courage:

Rachel was shy and didn't like talking to people in public. But while she was on a mission trip, she felt led by the Holy Spirit to tell the group her story. Rachel was scared, but she did what she was told and told her story. As she spoke, she felt calm and sure of herself, and her story had a big effect on those who heard it. Rachel overcame her fear of public speaking after this event and now gladly takes advantage of chances to share her faith.

These different events show how the Holy Spirit guides, comforts, inspires and changes each person's life in a unique way. If we stay open and aware of His presence, we can experience the fullness of a connection with the Holy Spirit in deeply personal and life-changing ways.

When you fully accept the Holy Spirit's presence, a deep change takes place in every part of your life. This power to change things isn't just a small tweak; it has a big impact on your heart, mind, and soul, making your life richer and more meaningful.

When you embrace the Holy Spirit, one of the first changes you experience is an enhanced sense of peace. Philippians 4:7 speaks of "the peace of God, which transcends all understanding," and this peace guards your heart and mind. The Holy Spirit calms your anxieties and fears, replacing them with a deep-seated tranquility that persists even amid life's storms. This peace is not dependent on external circumstances but is a steady assurance of God's presence and sovereignty.

The Holy Spirit also brings clarity and wisdom, guiding you through life's complexities. James 1:5 assures us that if we lack wisdom, we can ask God, who gives generously. The Holy Spirit illuminates your path, helping you discern right from wrong and make decisions that align with God's will. This divine guidance leads to better choices and fewer regrets as you begin to see situations from a heavenly perspective rather than through the limited lens of human understanding.

A fully embraced relationship with the Holy Spirit fosters a profound transformation in your character. Galatians 5:22-23 describes the fruit of the Spirit as love, joy, peace, forbearance, kindness, goodness, faithfulness, gentleness, and self-control. These attributes manifest more prominently in your life, affecting how you interact with others and handle challenges. You become more patient, compassionate, and forgiving, reflecting Christ's love in your relationships. This character transformation benefits you and impacts those around you, drawing them closer to the love of Christ.

Embracing the Holy Spirit also ignites a passion for prayer and worship. Prayer becomes more than a ritual; it becomes a heartfelt conversation with God. You begin to experience deeper and more intimate worship times, where the Holy Spirit moves and speaks to you. These moments of communion strengthen your bond with God, filling you with His presence and power. Worship becomes a lifestyle where every action and decision is an act of reverence and gratitude toward God.

The Holy Spirit empowers you to live out your faith boldly and share the gospel with others. Acts 1:8 declares, "But you will receive power when the Holy Spirit comes on you, and you will be my witnesses." This empowerment gives you the courage to step out of your comfort zone, whether sharing your testimony, serving in ministry, or standing up for justice. The Holy Spirit equips you with the necessary gifts and abilities to fulfill your God-given purpose, enabling you to significantly impact the world.

The Holy Spirit cultivates a deeper understanding and love for God's Word. Scriptures come alive as the Holy Spirit teaches and reveals their meanings to you. This deeper understanding transforms your thinking, aligning your thoughts with God's truths. Romans 12:2 encourages us to be transformed by the renewing of our minds, and the Holy Spirit plays a crucial role in this renewal. You begin to see the world through the lens of God's Word, shaping your worldview and responses to life's challenges.

The transformative power of the Holy Spirit also brings healing and freedom. Whether it's emotional wounds, destructive habits, or spiritual bondage, the Holy Spirit works to bring wholeness and liberty. 2 Corinthians 3:17 states, "Where the Spirit of the Lord is, there is freedom." This freedom allows you to live without the chains of past hurts or present struggles, embracing a life of victory and joy.

Baptism in the Holy Spirit

Baptism in the Holy Spirit is a profound and transformative experience that deepens one's relationship with God and empowers believers to live out their faith more fully. Unlike water baptism, which symbolizes cleansing and rebirth, baptism in the Holy Spirit refers to being filled with the Holy Spirit's power and presence.

This experience is often marked by an increased awareness of God's presence, a deeper sense of spiritual authority, and the activation of spiritual gifts. In Acts 1:8, Jesus promises His disciples, "But you will receive power when the Holy Spirit comes on you, and you will be my witnesses in Jerusalem, and in all Judea and Samaria, and to the ends of the earth." This power enables believers to witness boldly, serve effectively, and live a life that reflects the character and mission of Jesus.

The baptism can occur at any point in a believer's journey, sometimes immediately after conversion and other times later in their walk with God. It is not a one-time event but the beginning of a dynamic and ongoing relationship with the Holy Spirit. It enriches prayer life, enhances worship, and brings a deeper understanding of the Scriptures. It also often includes the manifestation of spiritual gifts such as prophecy, speaking in tongues, healing, and discernment, which are given for the edification of the church and the fulfillment of God's purposes.

To seek baptism in the Holy Spirit, one needs to approach God with an open and willing heart, asking Him to fill and empower them. The Holy Spirit is given freely to those who ask in faith, as Jesus assures in Luke 11:13, "If you then, though you are evil, know how to give good gifts to your children, how much more will your Father in heaven give the Holy Spirit to those who ask him!"

Prayer for Baptism in the Holy Spirit

Heavenly Father,

I come before You in the name of Jesus Christ, Your Son. I thank You for the gift of salvation and for cleansing me of my sins. I now ask You to fill me with the Holy Spirit and baptize me with Your power, presence, and love. I desire to live a life that glorifies You, to serve You faithfully, and to witness boldly to others about Your grace and truth.

Holy Spirit, I invite You into every area of my life. Empower me with Your gifts, guide me with Your wisdom, and transform me with Your presence. Help me to hear Your voice clearly and to follow Your leading. I surrender my will to You and ask that You fill me to overflowing.

Thank You, Lord, for this precious gift. I receive it by faith and commit to walking in the fullness of Your Spirit. In Jesus' name, I pray.

Amen.

When you accept the baptism in the Holy Spirit, your spiritual life gets deeper and stronger. It's an invitation to get to know God better and be better able to serve Him in deep ways. As you look for and accept this baptism, may the Holy

Spirit's power, wisdom, and love fill you, giving you a new sense of purpose and passion for your faith.

Every person should demonstrate that the old self is dead and that they now have a new life with Jesus Christ. You are now born of the spirit. Changes will begin to occur only if you allow them. Start listening for his guidance so he may direct you. Find a quiet space; you won't be able to hear his voice if there is too much noise.

Chapter 3: Growing Stronger in Your Faith

Renewing your mind is crucial for spiritual growth because it transforms how you perceive the world, yourself, and your relationship with God. This transformation involves acquiring knowledge and internalizing truths that reshape your thoughts, attitudes, and actions. Let's explore why renewing your mind is essential and how it manifests in everyday life.

It aligns your thoughts with God's will. Romans 12:2 says, "Do not conform to the pattern of this world but be transformed by renewing your mind. Then you can test and approve God's will—His good, pleasing, and perfect will." When your mind is renewed, you begin to see life from God's perspective, making choices that reflect His desires for you.

Our minds can be trapped in negative thinking patterns, such as fear, anxiety, or self-doubt. By renewing your mind, you can break free from these destructive cycles. For example, if you constantly worry about the future, refreshing your mind involves replacing those anxious thoughts with trust in God's provision and care, as stated in Philippians 4:6-7.

It's important to remember that spiritual maturity is a continuous process. As you grow in understanding and applying God's Word, your spiritual discernment improves.

Hebrews 5:14 notes that mature believers "have their powers of discernment trained by constant practice to distinguish good from evil."

Think of a garden overtaken by weeds. If left unattended, the weeds will choke out the healthy plants. Similarly, if we allow negative, worldly thoughts to dominate our minds, they will hinder our spiritual growth. Renewing your mind is like regularly weeding the garden, removing harmful thoughts, and cultivating the truth of God's Word.

Another example is a computer that has accumulated too many unnecessary files, slowing its performance. Just as a computer needs regular maintenance to run efficiently, our minds need constant renewal to focus on what matters most. By renewing our minds, we can clear out the clutter and distractions that prevent us from experiencing the fullness of life in Christ.

Imagine you are driving a car that is out of alignment. It constantly pulls to one side, making it challenging to stay on course. Renewing your mind is like getting a spiritual alignment. It ensures that your thoughts, beliefs, and attitudes are aligned with God's truth, enabling you to stay on the path He has set for you.

Consider the story of a young man named John who struggled with feelings of inadequacy and fear of failure. Whenever he faced a challenge, his mind was filled with thoughts like "I'm not good enough" or "I can't do this." These thoughts paralyzed him, preventing him from stepping out in faith. However, John decided to renew his mind by immersing himself in God's Word. He memorized scriptures like Philippians 4:13, "I can do all things through Christ who strengthens me," and Romans 8:37, "In all these things, we are more than conquerors through Him who loved us." Over time, these truths began to replace the negative thoughts. John's confidence grew, and he started to see himself as God sees him—capable, loved, and empowered.

Renewing your mind also involves guarding what you allow into it. Just as you wouldn't fill your body with junk food and expect to be healthy, you can't fill your mind with negative, worldly influences and hope to grow spiritually. Philippians 4:8 advises us to consider whatever is true, noble, correct, pure, lovely, admirable, excellent, or praiseworthy. Focusing on these things feeds your mind with what nurtures spiritual growth.

Consider another example: an athlete training for a marathon. To perform well, the athlete must follow a disciplined exercise regimen, nutrition, and rest. Similarly, renewing your mind requires discipline. It involves regularly reading and meditating on Scripture, praying, and seeking fellowship with other believers. This spiritual discipline strengthens your mind and spirit, preparing you to run the race of faith with endurance.

Imagine a sculptor working on a block of marble. The sculptor chips away at the stone, gradually revealing a beautiful statue. In the same way, renewing your mind is a process of chipping away at the falsehoods and negative patterns until the beauty of Christ is revealed in you. This process takes time and patience, but the result is a mind that reflects the character and wisdom of God.

The transformation from renewing your mind is evident in your interactions with others. When your mind is filled with God's truth, you respond to situations with love, patience, and wisdom. You become a light in a dark world, reflecting the grace and truth of Jesus Christ. This transformation benefits you and impacts those around you, drawing them closer to God.

It is also crucial for spiritual growth because it changes how you think, feel, and act. By aligning your thoughts with God's will, breaking free from negative patterns, and continuously growing in spiritual maturity, you experience a deeper, more fulfilling relationship with God. This ongoing process requires discipline, patience, and a commitment to filling your mind with the truths of God's Word. As you renew your mind, you will see the transformation in your life, becoming more like Christ and living out His purposes with confidence and joy.

Renewing your mind and deepening your faith requires intentional effort, especially amid a busy modern lifestyle. Here are some practical, doable steps to help you grow spiritually while managing your daily responsibilities:

1. Start Your Day with Prayer:

Begin each day with a brief prayer, dedicating the day to God. This can be as simple as saying, "Lord, guide me today and help me to reflect Your love in everything I do." It sets a positive tone for the day and keeps you focused on God's presence.

2. Incorporate Scripture into Your Routine:

Use a Bible app to read a verse or a short devotional each morning. Many apps offer notifications, reminding you to focus on God's Word for a few moments. You can also listen to audio versions of the Bible during your commute or while doing household chores.

3. Practice Gratitude:

Take a moment to reflect on three things you are grateful for each day. This practice helps shift your focus from stress and negativity to recognizing God's blessings. Consider keeping a gratitude journal to document these reflections.

4. Set Reminders for Prayer:

Use your phone or a watch to set daily alarms as reminders to pray. These can be quick prayers, such as thanking God for a meal, asking for guidance during a meeting, or seeking patience in a challenging moment.

5. Join a Small Group or Bible Study:

Find a small group or Bible study that fits your schedule, whether it's once a week or biweekly. Connecting with others provides accountability and encouragement. Many churches offer online groups, which can be more convenient for a busy lifestyle.

6. Memorize Scripture:

Choose one Bible verse each week to memorize. Write it on a sticky note and place it where you'll see it often, such as on your bathroom mirror, computer screen, or refrigerator. Repeating the verse throughout the week helps internalize God's Word.

7. Integrate Worship into Your Day:

Listen to worship music while driving, exercising, or working. Singing along or simply reflecting on the lyrics can be a form of prayer and keeps your mind focused on God.

8. Pray with Others:

Take opportunities to pray with family, friends, or colleagues. This can be as simple as praying with your spouse before bed, saying grace with your family at meals, or having a quick prayer with a coworker before a big project.

9. Read Christian Books or Articles:

Set aside time to read books or articles that inspire and challenge your faith. Even 10-15 minutes a day can make a difference. If finding time to read is difficult, consider listening to audiobooks.

10. Serve Others:

Look for small ways to serve others daily, such as helping a neighbor, volunteering at your church, or offering a listening ear to someone in need. These acts of kindness reflect love and deepen your faith.

11. Practice Sabbath Rest:

Dedicate one day a week or a portion of a day to rest and focus on God. Use this time to unplug from work, spend time with family, and reflect on your spiritual journey. It helps you recharge and realign your priorities with God's.

12. Meditate on God's Promises:

Take a few minutes each day to meditate on specific promises from the Bible. Close your eyes, breathe deeply, and let these truths sink into your heart. Verses like Jeremiah 29:11 and Philippians 4:13 can be incredibly encouraging.

13. Develop a Habit of Confession:

Regularly confess your sins to God, seeking His forgiveness and strength to overcome weaknesses. This practice keeps your heart humble and open to the Holy Spirit's transformative work.

14. Utilize Technology:

Leverage technology to support your spiritual growth. Use apps for daily devotionals, listen to Christian podcasts, join online prayer groups, and engage with faith-based social media content.

15. Reflect on Your Day:

Before bed, take a few moments to reflect on your day. Thank God for His blessings, identify areas where you fell short, and seek His guidance for tomorrow. This nightly reflection fosters a continuous dialogue with God.

Incorporating these practical steps into your busy lifestyle can deepen your faith and experience spiritual growth. These actions don't require large amounts of time but can have a significant impact when practiced consistently. Remember, the goal is to maintain a steady connection with God throughout your daily life, allowing His presence to guide and transform you.

Addressing Common Doubts and Questions

Question 1: Why Do I Struggle to Feel God's Presence?

Answer: Feeling God's presence can be challenging, especially in difficult times or when life gets busy. It's important to remember that God's presence isn't based on our feelings but on His promise.

He assures us in Hebrews 13:5, "I will never leave you nor forsake you." Sometimes, we might not feel His presence due to distractions, unconfessed sin, or simply because our faith is being tested.

Encouragement: Trust that God is with you even when you don't feel Him. Make time to quiet your mind, pray, and read His Word. Surround yourself with a supportive faith community and seek spiritual guidance. Faith often involves trusting in what we cannot see or feel (2 Corinthians 5:7).

Question 2: How Can I Know God's Will for My Life?

Answer: Discerning God's will can seem daunting, but He has given us tools to understand His plans. The Bible is our primary guide, with principles and examples of God's will. Prayer is also crucial, as it aligns our hearts with His. Additionally, God often speaks through circumstances and the counsel of wise, godly people.

Encouragement: James 1:5 encourages us to ask God for wisdom, promising He will give it generously. Be patient and open, seeking His guidance through prayer, Scripture, and community. Remember, God's will is often revealed step by step rather than in a precise moment. Trust in His timing and faithfulness.

Question 3: Why Does God Allow Suffering?

Answer: Suffering is one of the most challenging aspects of life to understand. We must recognize that we live in a fallen world where sin and its consequences affect everyone. God allows free will, which means people can choose actions that result in suffering. However, He also promises to use all things, including suffering, for the good of those who love Him (Romans 8:28).

Encouragement: God is with us in our suffering, offering comfort and strength. Jesus experienced great suffering and can empathize with our pain (Hebrews 4:15).

Lean on God during tough times, knowing He can bring growth, perseverance, and even blessings out of hardship. Seek support from your church and be open about your struggles.

Question 4: What If I Don't Feel Worthy of God's Love?

Answer: Many struggle with feelings of unworthiness, but God's love is not based on our merit. Romans 5:8 says, "But God demonstrates His love for us in this: While we were still sinners, Christ died for us." His love is unconditional and not something we earn but receive by grace.

Encouragement: Remember that you are created in God's image and are precious to Him (Genesis 1:27). His love for you is steadfast and unwavering.

When you struggle with feelings of unworthiness, remind yourself of God's truth and promises. Surround yourself with affirming and loving people who can help reinforce these truths.

Question 5: How Can I Strengthen My Faith When I Feel Weak?

Answer: Feeling weak in faith is a shared experience, especially during trials. Strengthening your faith involves regular spiritual disciplines like prayer, Bible study, and fellowship with other believers. Worship and service can also boost your faith by focusing on God's greatness and His work in and through you.

Encouragement: 2 Corinthians 12:9 reminds us that our weakness makes God's power perfect. When you feel weak, lean on God's strength. Be honest with Him about your struggles and seek His help. Faith can be as small as a mustard seed but still powerful enough to move mountains (Matthew 17:20).

Question 6: Why Don't My Prayers Seem to Be Answered?

Answer: Unanswered prayers can be discouraging, but it's essential to understand that God's ways are higher than ours (Isaiah 55:8-9). Sometimes, His answers come in ways we don't expect, or the timing is different from what we desire. Other times, God's response may be "no" or "wait" because He has a better plan.

Encouragement: Keep praying and trust that God hears you. Be open to the possibility that His answers may differ from your expectations. Reflect on how God has answered prayers in the past and remain hopeful. Sometimes, unanswered prayers teach us patience, trust, and reliance on God's wisdom.

Question 7: Can I Be Forgiven for My Past?

Answer: Yes, God's forgiveness is complete and total. 1 John 1:9 assures us, "If we confess our sins, He is faithful and just and will forgive us and purify us from all unrighteousness." No sin is too great for God's grace. Jesus' sacrifice on the cross covers all sins, past, present, and future.

Encouragement: Accepting God's forgiveness means also forgiving yourself. Let go of past guilt and embrace the new life God offers. Engage in regular confession and repentance, and seek accountability from trusted friends or mentors. Celebrate your freedom in Christ and live in the light of His grace.

Question 8: How Do I Handle Doubts About My Faith?

Answer: Doubt is a natural part of faith. Even firm believers experience moments of doubt. It's essential to confront doubts rather than ignore them. Study the Bible, ask questions, and seek answers. Engage with mature Christians who can provide wisdom and perspective.

Encouragement: Mark 9:24 records a man saying to Jesus, "I believe; help my unbelief!" This honest admission can be a powerful prayer. Use doubt as a catalyst for deeper exploration and understanding. Remember, faith is a journey, and God is patient with us as we grow.

Addressing these common doubts and questions with honesty and encouragement can help you find strength and reassurance in your spiritual journey. Embrace these struggles as opportunities to deepen your faith, knowing that God is with you every step of the way.

Practical Techniques for Reading and Understanding the Bible

Reading and understanding the Bible can be scary, but knowing how to do it right can be a beneficial and life-changing practice. Here are some excellent ways to do it.

Begin with prayer: Say a prayer before you read the Bible and ask God to help you understand what it says. This makes the reading more spiritual and asks the Holy Spirit to lead you. A short prayer, "Lord, help me see the wonderful truths in Your Word," can make a big difference.

Pick a Translation That Can Be Read: Choose a book of the Bible that is simple to understand. The New International Version (NIV), the New Living Translation (NLT), and the English Standard Version (ESV) make the text easier to understand without changing its truth. Reading will be more fun and less complicated if you can easily understand the translation.

Set Doable Goals: Make reading the Bible a goal that you can reach. Don't try to read big chunks all at once; start with small pieces you can handle. You could start with a specific book or part of the Bible every day. Reading regularly for shorter amounts of time can have a more enormous effect than reading for long periods on occasion.

Use a Bible or Study Guide: Study books and devotionals can help you understand things better. They often explain the passages, give historical information, and show how they can be used in real life. You could use a study Bible with notes or Oswald Chambers' book "My Utmost for His Highest."

Very Important: Context: Understanding the background of a passage is essential. Read the beginning of a book to learn about the author, the people who wrote it, and its goal. Understanding the historical and cultural background helps you understand what is being said and avoid getting it wrong.

Active reading is essential: Highlight, underline or note the text to get involved with it. List any questions, comments, or ideas that come to mind. This hands-on method helps you remember what you read and makes you think more deeply about it.

Think and meditate: After reading something, give yourself some time to think about what it means and how it can help you in your life. Think about important texts by repeating them to yourself. Psalm 1:2 says to enjoy the Lord's word and think about it all day and night. This helps you take the Bible seriously and use it daily.

Use what you've learned: You can't just read the Bible; it's also a way to live. As you read, think about how the things it says can help you in real life. James 1:22 tells us to put the Word into action, not just listen to it. Using the Bible makes it important and life-changing.

Join a group that studies the Bible: Being a part of a Bible study group gives you friends, responsibility, and different points of view. Talking about the Bible with others can help you understand it better and give you new ideas you might not have thought of on your own. There are groups at many churches, and you can also find them online.

Use tools and apps for the Bible: Use technology to help you read the Bible better. Apps like **You Version** let you choose from different reading plans, audio versions, and daily devotionals. You can access commentaries, lexicons, and many versions through tools like Blue Letter Bible or Bible Gateway.

Recall the Bible verses: When you need to remember God's Word, memorizing verses can help. Start with texts that speak to you or help you grow in areas where you want to. Reading and repeating your memory verses over and over will help them stick in your mind and heart.

Keep trying and being patient: It takes time to understand the Bible; it's not a race. Be kind to yourself and keep at what you're doing. There will be complex parts, but don't give up. It will take time for you to understand and appreciate it more.

Ask mature believers for help: Don't hesitate to ask pastors, teachers, or friends who know a lot for help. They can give you information, explain things, suggest tools, and cheer you on. Learning from other people's stories can make reading the Bible more meaningful.

Using these tips will make reading the Bible less scary and more enjoyable. If you read the Bible with an open mind and heart, you will find that it applies to your life and has power. This will strengthen your faith and your bond with God.

Putting what the Bible says to use in everyday life: When you use biblical lessons in real life, you must bridge the gap between old knowledge and new problems. Here are some steps to make the Bible helpful in your daily life and get help, comfort, and strength from it.

Understanding the Core Principles: Biblical teachings often revolve around core principles such as love, forgiveness, humility, integrity, and faith. Identifying these principles helps apply them universally, regardless of the situation. For example, Jesus' commandment to love your neighbor (Matthew 22:39) can guide interactions in any context, from family relationships to workplace dynamics.

Relating to Modern Scenarios

1. Dealing with Conflict: The Bible teaches us to handle conflict with grace and forgiveness. Matthew 18:15-17 outlines a process for addressing grievances directly and privately, seeking reconciliation. When dealing with conflicts in modern contexts, it is important to approach them with a spirit of resolution and understanding rather than aggression or avoidance.

2. Managing Stress and Anxiety: Philippians 4:6-7 encourages us not to be anxious but to present our requests to God through prayer and thanksgiving, promising that His peace will guard our hearts and minds. Make prayer and gratitude part of your stress management routine in today's fast-paced world. Whenever you feel overwhelmed, pause to pray and list things you're thankful for.

3. Making Ethical Decisions: Proverbs 3:5- 6 advises us to trust the Lord and not lean on our understanding. In making ethical decisions, seek God's guidance through prayer and Scripture. Reflect on whether your choices align with biblical values like honesty, integrity, and compassion.

4. Building Relationships: Ephesians 4:32 encourages kindness, compassion, and forgiveness. Apply this by actively listening to others, offering help without expecting anything in return, and being quick to forgive. Practice empathy and understanding in friendships, marriages, and professional relationships.

5. Facing Temptation: 1 Corinthians 10:13 assures us that God will provide a way out of temptation. Recognize your weaknesses and avoid situations that might lead you astray. When facing temptation, seek support from trusted friends or mentors, and remember that seeking God's help is always the first step.

6. Pursuing Justice: Micah 6:8 calls us to act justly, love mercy, and walk humbly with God. Apply this by standing up against injustice, advocating for those who cannot speak for themselves, and showing compassion and kindness in your interactions. This might involve community service, supporting fair practices, or being a voice for the marginalized.

Reflecting on Personal Experiences

Consider how biblical teachings have already impacted your life. Reflect on when applying Scripture brought peace, resolved a conflict, or guided a difficult decision. These reflections reinforce the Bible's relevance and provide a personal blueprint for future applications.

Practical Steps for Application

1. Daily Devotions: Start your day with a devotional time that includes reading Scripture, prayer, and reflection. This helps set a spiritual tone for the day, making you more mindful of applying biblical principles.

2. Journaling: Keep a journal to document how you apply biblical teachings in your life. Write about challenges, how you turned to Scripture for guidance, and the outcomes. This practice helps you see patterns of God's faithfulness and grow in your application skills.

3. Setting Reminders: Use reminders or sticky notes with Bible verses related to your working areas. Place them where you'll see them often—on your desk, mirror, or car dashboard. These visual cues keep biblical principles at the top of my mind throughout the day.

4. Role Models: Identify role models who exemplify living out biblical teachings. Learn from their experiences, seek their advice, and observe how they integrate faith into everyday life. These role models could be mentors, pastors, or even historical Christian figures.

5. Community Involvement: Engage in church activities, small groups, or volunteer opportunities. Being part of a faith community provides support, accountability, and practical examples of applying Scripture in various contexts.

6. Continuous Learning: Invest time in learning more about the Bible and its application. Attend workshops, read books, and participate in Bible studies. The more you understand the Bible's historical and cultural context, the better you can apply its teachings today.

Examples of Bridging the Gap

1. Workplace Integrity: Joseph's story in Genesis demonstrates maintaining integrity despite challenges. Apply this by being honest in your work, not cutting corners, and standing firm in ethical dilemmas. Reflect on Joseph's perseverance and faithfulness in every task, big or small.

2. Family Relationships: The story of Ruth and Naomi showcases loyalty and care within family dynamics. Apply this by being supportive and loving to family members, especially in tough times. Like Ruth, commit to being present and dependable for your loved ones.

3. Financial Stewardship: Proverbs 21:20 advises wise resource management. Apply this by budgeting wisely, saving, avoiding unnecessary debt, and being generous. View your finances as a responsibility of stewardship, making decisions that honor God.

4. Community Engagement: Jesus' parable of the Good Samaritan (Luke 10:25-37) teaches us to love and serve our neighbors. Apply this by helping those in need, showing kindness to strangers, and being part of your community. Look for opportunities to volunteer and support local initiatives.

5. Health and Well-Being: 1 Corinthians 6:19-20 reminds us that our bodies are temples of the Holy Spirit. Apply this by caring for your physical health through proper nutrition, exercise, and rest. Consider your body's care as part of your spiritual discipline.

By integrating these techniques and examples, you can effectively apply biblical teachings to real-life situations, making Scripture a living and active guide for today's challenges. Through prayer, reflection, and practical actions, the wisdom of the Bible can transform your life, leading you to greater spiritual maturity and fulfillment.

Community is an integral part of growing in faith because it provides a solid base for spiritual growth and support. In a world that values independence highly, the biblical model of community strikes a strong balance that shows how important it is to connect with others, help each other, and grow together.

Being a part of a group of believers has many benefits for growing and strengthening one's faith. For starters, it makes people responsible. There is a feeling of duty to uphold the values and principles of the trust when you are with other believers. This holds people accountable for their spiritual journey and encourages them to live out their faith genuinely and regularly. The group also offers support during tough times. Life is full of problems, and dealing with them alone can make you feel lonely and hopeless. When you're in a religious community that supports you, you have a group of people who can offer comfort, prayer, and practical help when things get complicated. This kind of group support can make a big difference in how well someone can keep going and keep their hope.

In a group, learning and growth are also significantly boosted. Each person brings their ideas, experiences, and readings of the Bible to the group. Together, they help everyone understand the Bible better and in more depth. People can learn from each other, ask questions, and explore their faith more deeply and collaboratively when participating in group studies, talks, and worship services.

The community helps people feel like they fit in and are who they are. When you join a faith group, you connect with something bigger than yourself. There is a spiritual family where people can find love, acceptance, and a reason to live. Belonging is essential for spiritual health because it helps people see how they fit into God's bigger plan and goal.

The community promotes service and reaching out. There are more chances to help others and follow Jesus' teachings when you're with a group that supports you. As a community member, you are encouraged to look beyond yourself and make a positive difference in the world, whether it's through planned church events, mission trips, or random acts of kindness.

A group gives people with doubts or questions about their faith a safe place to discuss them. Other Christians can offer comfort, talk about their problems, and share what they've learned from their experiences. Being open and vulnerable in a community can be healing and reassuring, helping people deal with their doubts with kindness and support.

Finding and committing to a faith group in today's busy and often disconnected world can be complex. But the benefits are much more significant than the work. The relationships in these places are beneficial, whether through a church, a small group, or an online fellowship. They give you the spiritual food, support, and guidance you need to grow your faith.

It is important to tell readers to find and spend time with other Christians who can help them. It's a call to get out of being alone and into relationships that help you grow spiritually. In this way, people grow in their faith and help others in the community grow and become stronger. Following the biblical model of community strengthens the body of Christ and makes each person more able to handle hardships in their faith.

It is essential to use discernment when choosing spiritual direction and community. The people we hang out with significantly impact our faith journey. That's why it is essential to find leaders and groups that follow biblical principles and help people grow spiritually.

It takes careful thought and prayer to choose a spiritual direction. It's essential to look for leaders and teachers who have a strong relationship with God, are good people, and know the Bible inside and out. These people should live out their faith and be willing to walk with you, giving you biblically-based advice and support. Discernment helps you find people who want to help you grow spiritually, not people who might lead you astray with teachings or practices not in the Bible. Judgment is crucial to finding a group supporting your faith when looking for friends. A healthy faith group should be based on the Bible, create an atmosphere of love and support, and push its members to grow closer to God. It is essential to be a part of a group whose lessons align with biblical teaching and whose members all promise to follow the faith's rules.

Staying rooted in prayer and the Bible is important to make intelligent decisions. Regularly asking God for help and reading His Word gives you the knowledge and understanding you need to make smart choices. The Holy Spirit is important in this process because He gives you ideas and beliefs that help you find the right spiritual leaders and groups.

Being part of a group that values wisdom can also help you make intelligent decisions. Other Christians who are also seeking God's will can offer helpful insights and suggestions. Their life experiences and insights can help you figure out how to find spiritual direction and community.

It's ultimately important to surround yourself with things that bring you closer to God and help you grow in your faith. If you find the right spiritual direction and community, they will push you to learn more about the Bible, be there for you when things get hard, and be happy when things go well. They will hold you responsible, pray for and with you, and go on your spiritual journey.

Trust that God will lead you to the right people and communities as you use your discernment to pick spiritual direction and community. If you stay open to His guidance and determined to do what He wants, you can find the support and motivation you need to grow in your faith. This discernment protects your spiritual health and helps you find essential relationships that can change your life.

God's Favor

I ask God to allow Mike, my son, to bring me to Tennessee to see this lady in the old folk's home. From what her son says, the weather was so bad; there was a snowstorm when I was supposed to arrive. Instead, it was clear, and the ice was hanging on the mountain, which made it more beautiful and a clear and sunny day. The lord cleared it up, so I don't have any problems obeying his call because it was not supposed to be clear like that. Her son said she was all twisted up, but when I got there, God healed her. When I arrived, she was sitting in a wheelchair, waiting for me to arrive. The Holy Spirit went before me and healed her. Praise be to God!

Chapter 4: Living Fully with the Holy Spirit

A key part of living a spiritual life is recognizing the Holy Spirit's leading in all of life's events, from big decisions to small ones. The Holy Spirit is our spiritual leader and helps us make decisions in every part of our lives. This advice can be very subtle but has a big effect, helping us get through the complicated parts of daily life with peace and clarity.

Being open and sensitive is the first step in tuning in to the Holy Spirit. When we pray and meditate regularly, we can hear the Holy Spirit's words more clearly. We are more open to His soft promptings when we take time to think and pray. By doing this, we get better at noticing the small signs that the Holy Spirit sends to help us follow Him.

When making big choices, like picking a job path, buying something important, or thinking about making a big change in your life, asking the Holy Spirit for help is important. To begin, talk to God about your worries and questions. Tell the Holy Spirit what you want and are afraid of, and then ask him to show you the best way to move forward. Often, the Holy Spirit makes things clear by giving people a sense of peace when they make a choice. This peace is a strong sign that you are doing what God wants you to do. On the other hand, if a choice makes you feel uneasy or worried, the Holy Spirit may be telling you to think again.

The Bible is a way for the Holy Spirit to guide us. When we read the Bible regularly, the Holy Spirit brings to our attention parts that speak directly to our lives. For example, when you are worried about money, you might read a verse that makes you feel better about God's care. These events are not random; they are signs that the Holy Spirit uses God's Word to guide your steps. It can be helpful to write down these Bible verses because they help you remember how the Holy Spirit has led you through different stages of your life.

The Holy Spirit's help is just as important when making smaller, more everyday choices. Even though these decisions may not seem important, they greatly impact our lives and who we are as people. In these times, an inner prompting or conviction can help you figure out where the Holy Spirit is leading you. For instance, you might want to get in touch with a friend you haven't talked to in a while, only to find that they really need some support. These nudges are the Holy Spirit's way of setting up divine meetings where God's love and care can reach you.

Another aspect of recognizing the Holy Spirit's guidance is the presence of peace and joy. The fruits of the Spirit, as described in Galatians 5:22-23, include love, joy, peace, patience, kindness, goodness, faithfulness, gentleness, and self-control. When a decision or action aligns with these fruits, it is often a sign of the Holy Spirit's leading. For instance, if you are contemplating a response to a difficult situation and the approach that brings peace and kindness comes to mind, it is likely the Holy Spirit guiding you to act in a way that reflects Christ's character.

The Holy Spirit also uses circumstances and the counsel of others to guide us. Sometimes, the doors that open or close in our lives are indicators of the Holy Spirit's direction. Pay attention to these circumstances and seek to discern their meaning through prayer. Additionally, God places wise and godly people in our lives to offer counsel. When faced with a decision, seeking the advice of trusted spiritual mentors can help clarify the Holy Spirit's guidance. These individuals can provide perspective and wisdom that align with God's will, helping you make informed and Spirit-led choices.

It often speaks through a still, small voice—a gentle whisper that we must be attentive to hear. Elijah experienced this in 1 Kings 19:12, where God said to him not in the wind, earthquake, or fire but in a gentle whisper. This teaches us that the Holy Spirit's guidance is often quiet and requires us to be still and listen. In our fast-paced world, cultivating moments of silence and stillness can help us better hear and recognize this gentle voice.

This advice is sometimes clear after the fact. If you remember the choices you made and how they turned out, you can see how the Holy Spirit was leading you, even if you didn't know it at the time. Thinking about these events helps you accept that the Holy Spirit is always with you and guiding you.

As Christians, being aware of the Holy Spirit's guidance changes how we make choices, both big and small. We are told to live on purpose and always try to ensure our deeds align with God's will. We become more sensitive to the Holy Spirit's guidance when we pray, read the Bible, pay attention to our inner voices, and are open to the advice of others. Being aware helps us handle the tricky parts of life with understanding, peace, and trust since we know the Holy Spirit guides us in every choice.

When you use the Holy Spirit to help you make important choices, you need to combine spiritual knowledge with common sense to ensure your choices align with God's will and are useful in your daily life. This useful method has several important steps:

- Prayer.

- Studying the Bible to make decisions.

- Getting advice from a godly person.

- Watching the situation, following your gut feelings.

- Thinking about peace and conviction.

Prayer and Seeking God's Guidance

The foundation of any decision-making process as a believer begins with prayer. Bring your concerns and decisions before God, asking for the Holy Spirit's guidance. Pray for wisdom, clarity, and the ability to discern God's will. James 1:5 assures us that if we ask for wisdom, God will generously provide it. Prayer aligns our hearts with God and opens us to His guidance. Set aside specific times for focused prayer regarding the decision at hand, and be persistent, knowing that God hears and responds to our requests.

Discernment Through Scripture

The Bible is one of the best places to get knowledge and direction. Reading the Bible regularly lets the Holy Spirit shine a light on parts that can point you in the right way. When you have to make a big choice, read the appropriate Bible verses and ask the Holy Spirit to show you how they apply to your case. The Bible often gives us morals that can help us make choices, like being honest, having patience, and trusting God. For those times when the Bible lines really hit you, the Holy Spirit may be speaking to you through them. Write them down in a journal.

Seeking Godly Counsel

Proverbs 15:22 states, "Plans fail for lack of counsel, but with many advisers they succeed." Seeking advice from trusted, godly individuals can provide valuable perspective and wisdom. Choose mentors, spiritual leaders, or mature Christians who have demonstrated discernment and wisdom in their own lives. Discuss your situation with them, listen to their insights, and weigh their advice carefully. God often speaks through the counsel of others, providing clarity and confirmation through their experiences and understanding.

Observing Circumstances

Situations are often ways that the Holy Spirit leads us. As you think about your choice, pay attention to the chances and problems that come up. A door that is open or closed can show you where God wants you to go. For instance, if you are thinking about getting a new job and then all of a sudden get a chance that fits, that could be the Holy Spirit's direction. On the other hand, if more than one obstacle stands in the way of a road, it might be best to think again. But being smart is very important—some problems are supposed to be solved, so think about whether the problems are a test of your faith or a divine reroute.

Listening to Inner Promptings

Inner promptings, those soft nudges or feelings on your heart, are a common way that the Holy Spirit leads. These can be a calm feeling about a choice or a strong desire to go down a certain road or stay away from it. To hear these signals, make it a habit to be still and listen. Every day, make time to clear your thoughts and focus on God. During these times, pay attention to thoughts or feelings that come up over and over again. If you feel like you're always going in a certain direction, the Holy Spirit may be leading you.

Reflecting on Peace and Conviction

One of the key indicators of the Holy Spirit's guidance is a sense of peace. Colossians 3:15 advises us to "let the peace of Christ rule in your hearts." As you consider your options, reflect on which choice brings a deep, abiding peace. This peace is different from fleeting emotions; it is a settled assurance that you are on the right path. Additionally, pay attention to any strong convictions. If you feel a persistent unease or conviction about a particular choice, it may be the Holy Spirit cautioning you against it.

Integrating Spiritual Wisdom with Common Sense

Even though spiritual knowledge is very important, using it along with common sense makes sure that choices are useful and last. God often works through our smarts and logic. Think about the possible outcomes and effects when you're weighing your choices. Think about the long-term effects of each choice and make a list of the pros and cons. Using common sense means checking to see if the choice is in line with religious principles and will help you and other people.

Making the Decision and Trusting God

After praying about all of these things, make your choice with faith, believing that the Holy Spirit has led you. When you do something, you should have faith that God is with you. Remember that not every choice will be easy and that the Holy Spirit will sometimes lead us through a process of making mistakes. Trust that God will forgive us for our mistakes and lead us in the right direction if we need it. Give God your choice, and know that He will continue to guide you as you move forward.

These steps will help you make big decisions with spiritual insight and common sense, making sure that your choices are in line with God's will and what is best for you. With this balanced attitude, you can handle the challenges of life with peace and confidence, knowing that the Holy Spirit is leading you. Finding your God-given purpose and interests is a life-changing journey that requires you to understand your unique gifts and make sure they fit with God's plan for your life. This discovery not only makes you happy and fulfilled, but it also gives you a way to make a real difference in the world. Here are a few ways to start this journey to find your divine purpose and your true love.

Prayer and Reflection

Prayer and deep thought are the first steps to finding your God-given mission. Spend some time in quiet reflection, asking God to show you His plans for you and giving you advice. Prayer is a strong way to get in touch with God's will. Ask yourself, "What are my interests and skills?" and "How can I use them to help others and honor God?" Think about the things that have happened to you in your life; they may hold clues about your mission. Writing these thoughts down in a journal can help you see trends and new ideas that come up over time.

Understanding Your Talents and Gifts

Recognize that everyone has been blessed with unique talents and gifts. Romans 12:6- 8 emphasizes that we each have different gifts according to the grace given to us. Take an inventory of your skills and abilities. What activities come naturally to you? What do others often compliment you on? These talents are indicators of areas where God has equipped you to excel. Consider taking spiritual gifts assessments, which can provide insights into your strengths and how you can use them in ministry and service.

Exploring Your Passions

You're passionate about the things and issues that make you excited and happy. These things often show you where God wants you to make a change. Spend some time thinking about what makes you happy and excited. What do you really care about or need the most? Your interests can help you find your purpose by showing you where you can make a real difference. For instance, if you really want to help kids, you could find your purpose in teaching, being a guide, or speaking out for child welfare.

Seeking Guidance from Scripture

The Bible is a rich resource for understanding God's purposes for His people. Study passages that speak about calling and purpose. Verses like Jeremiah 29:11 reassure us that God has plans to prosper us and give us hope, and Ephesians 2:10, which states that we are created for good works, can provide encouragement and direction. Meditate on these scriptures, asking the Holy Spirit to illuminate their relevance to your life.

Engaging in Community and Fellowship

Being a part of a group of believers is important for finding your meaning. People who are also Christians can help, support, and guide you. Have honest conversations about your search for meaning with friends, mentors, and spiritual leaders you trust. They can give you useful advice and may see talents and interests in you that you don't see yourself. Volunteering in different ways at church or in the community can also help you figure out where you feel most satisfied and able to make a difference.

Trying New Things

To find your meaning, you may need to leave your comfort zone and try new things. Volunteers can help with different church or community projects or programs. Taking on new responsibilities and jobs can help you find talents and interests you didn't know you had. As you do different things, pay attention to where you feel most motivated and productive. You can get a better sense of your meaning through this process of exploration.

Listening to the Holy Spirit

The Holy Spirit leads and counsels us and helps us know what God wants for our lives. Prayer, worship, and meditation are all good ways to get in touch with the Holy Spirit. The Holy Spirit will gently push you in the right direction. Could you pay attention to them? God talks to us in subtle ways sometimes, and being aware of how He is leading us can lead to new chances and paths.

Reflecting on Life Experiences

Your experiences, both good and bad, can help you figure out your mission. Consider important events that have changed you. What events have given you the ability to understand how others feel or meet their precise needs? People's biggest interests often come from things that have caused them a lot of pain or joy. For example, someone who has been through a lot of struggle may feel driven to help others who are going through the same thing.

Embracing Your Unique Path

Realizing that your path is special and different from other people's is very important. God's plan for your life is unique and takes into account your traits, skills, and experiences. Please do not compare your path to others because it can make you feel down and take your attention away from your goal. Trust that God has a special place for you in His kingdom as you go on your unique journey.

Committing to Lifelong Learning and Growth

To find your meaning, you have to go on a journey that lasts your whole life. Make a promise to keep learning and growing, both personally and emotionally. Stay open to new things, learning, and growing as a person. Your idea of your meaning may change as you grow, which can lead to new chances and directions.

To sum up, to find your God-given purpose and passions, you need to pray, think, understand your talents, explore your passions, look for direction in the Bible, be a part of a community, try new things, listen to the Holy Spirit, think about your life experiences, accept your unique path, and make a promise to keep learning. By adding these habits to your routine, you can find your unique skills and make them fit with God's plan. This will help you live a full and meaningful life.

The Holy Spirit has the power to change relationships, from family relationships to friendships and love partnerships. By letting the Holy Spirit into our lives, we let God's love, knowledge, and direction shape how we treat other people, making our relationships healthier and more loving.

Family Dynamics

Family relationships are foundational and often the most complex. The Holy Spirit can bring harmony and understanding to family dynamics, healing old wounds and fostering a spirit of unity. One way the Holy Spirit transforms family relationships is by instilling a deep sense of forgiveness and grace. Colossians 3:13 encourages us to "bear with each other and forgive one another if any of you has a grievance against someone. Forgive as the Lord forgave you." This divine forgiveness helps family members let go of past hurts and build stronger bonds.

The Holy Spirit also promotes effective communication within families. Ephesians 4:29 advises us to speak in ways that build others up according to their needs. The Spirit can guide our words, helping us to communicate with kindness, patience, and love, reducing misunderstandings and conflicts. By fostering an environment of open, honest, and loving communication, the Holy Spirit helps create a more supportive and nurturing family atmosphere.

Moreover, the Holy Spirit can bring peace to families in times of conflict. When tensions arise, the Spirit can provide calm and wisdom, helping family members approach disagreements with a spirit of reconciliation rather than confrontation. This peace, as described in Philippians 4:7, transcends understanding and guards our hearts and minds, allowing us to resolve conflicts amicably and with mutual respect.

Friendships

Friendships are another area where the Holy Spirit can work powerfully. True, deep friendships reflect the love of Christ, and the Holy Spirit helps us embody this love. Galatians 5:22-23 lists the fruits of the Spirit, which include love, joy, peace, patience, kindness, goodness, faithfulness, gentleness, and self-control. These qualities are essential for nurturing and maintaining strong, healthy friendships.

The Holy Spirit encourages us to be loyal and supportive friends. Proverbs 17:17 says, "A friend loves at all times, and a brother is born for a time of adversity." The Spirit empowers us to be there for our friends, offering support and encouragement, especially during difficult times. This steadfast presence strengthens the bond of friendship and provides a tangible expression of God's love.

In addition, the Holy Spirit helps us to be empathetic and understanding. Romans 12:15 encourages us to "rejoice with those who rejoice; mourn with those who mourn." By helping us to share in our friends' joys and sorrows, the Holy Spirit deepens our connections and fosters genuine, compassionate relationships.

Romantic Partnerships

In romantic relationships, the Holy Spirit can transform how partners interact, leading to a deeper, more meaningful connection. One of the key ways the Holy Spirit impacts romantic relationships is by fostering selfless love. 1 Corinthians 13:4-7 describes love as patient, kind, and not self-seeking. The Holy Spirit helps us embody these qualities, encouraging us to prioritize our partner's needs and well-being above our own.

The Holy Spirit also plays a crucial role in promoting fidelity and commitment. Ephesians 5:25 calls on husbands to love their wives just as Christ loved the church and gave Himself up for her. This sacrificial love, inspired by the Holy

Spirit, strengthens the commitment between partners and helps them to remain faithful and devoted to one another.

The Holy Spirit's guidance can significantly improve communication in romantic relationships. The Spirit helps partners to speak truthfully and lovingly, fostering an environment of trust and openness.

Ephesians 4:15 emphasizes speaking the truth in love, which is essential for resolving conflicts and maintaining a healthy relationship.

The Holy Spirit helps people in a relationship grow spiritually together. The Spirit strengthens their spiritual bond and brings their relationship in line with God's will by pushing them to pray, study the Bible, and worship together. This spiritual journey strengthens their relationship and gives it a solid base.

It has the power to change ties in every part of life. The Spirit gives peace, forgiveness, and good communication to families. The Holy Spirit grows love, support, and understanding in friendships. When people are in a relationship, the Spirit encourages pure love, devotion, and spiritual growth.

We let God's love and knowledge guide us when we let the Holy Spirit into our relationships. This makes our relationships with others healthier and more satisfying. This change not only makes our relationships better, but it also shows the world God's love and kindness.

Major Breakthroughs by Following the Holy Spirit's Leading

Sarah's Career Transformation

Sarah had a good-paying job in a business, but she was unhappy and stressed at work. Even though her job gave her security, she felt a strong urge to take a different road. After hearing a talk at church one Sunday about following the Holy Spirit, Sarah was sure she had to make a change. To take a chance, she chose to pray, especially for help with her career.

Sarah asked the Holy Spirit to show her real calling over the next few weeks by spending a lot of time praying and meditating. During this time, she became more interested in schooling and wanted to work with kids. Sarah decided to go to a school to become a teacher, even though it meant taking a pay cut and not knowing what would happen next.

Just a few months after starting her new job, Sarah felt a deep sense of joy and meaning. She got a lot of satisfaction from shaping young minds, and she could see the good effects on her kids.

Her relationships with students and coworkers got stronger, and she felt more in line with God's plan for her life. Thanks to the guidance of the Holy Spirit, she found a job that fulfilled her and gave her a chance to help others in a worthwhile way.

Mark's Reconciliation with His Father

Because of fights and mistakes in the past, Mark's relationship with his father was tense for a long time. The unresolved stress made him feel bad, but he didn't reach out because he was afraid or proud.

One evening, while he was praying for direction and peace, Mark felt a strong push from the Holy Spirit to make peace with his father.

Mark did what he was told, even though he had doubts. He called his dad and asked if they could talk. He was shocked when his dad agreed. Mark told them how he felt and said sorry for his part in their arguments during their meeting. Mark's earnestness and humility moved his father, who also apologized for what he had done.

What they said to each other was the start of them both getting better. Their relationship got a lot better over time as they learned to accept and understand each other. The Holy Spirit's guidance not only fixed their relationship but also brought them a lot of peace and helped them heal emotionally.

Linda's Health Miracle

Linda had been sick for a long time and had been having a hard time. Even after many treatments and medications, her health didn't improve, and her faith started to waver. In the middle of a church service one day, the Holy Spirit strongly urged her to go to an evening prayer meeting for recovery.

Linda chose to go to the session even though she wasn't sure about it. Her feelings of peace and love during the prayer were like nothing she had ever felt before. The pastor prayed especially for her to get better, and Linda felt hopeful when she left the meeting.

Over the next few weeks, Linda's health changed dramatically. Her problems improved over time, and her doctors were shocked at how well she was doing. She strongly believed that she was healed because she listened to the Holy Spirit and went to pray. She saw the power of the Holy Spirit at work in her life, which strengthened her faith and improved her relationship with God.

James's Mission Trip Calling

James had a strong desire to serve God, but he didn't know how to do it. Before a mission-focused service at his church, he felt a strong urge from the Holy Spirit to go on a mission trip to a remote town in Africa. James was scared about this idea because he had never been abroad and didn't know what problems he might face.

James signed up for the trip even though he was scared. He chose to trust the Holy Spirit's leading. It was hard to get ready and raise money, but he had a deep sense of peace and confidence that he was on the right track.

When James arrived in Africa, he worked on several different projects, such as building schools and helping people get medical care.

James's life changed because of the event. He saw the huge difference their work made in the community and felt a huge sense of purpose and satisfaction. He knew he was called to social work because of the people he met and the lives he changed. After he got back home, James kept going on mission trips and became an advocate for his church's world outreach. He saw a new way to serve, and his faith grew stronger because the Holy Spirit led him.

Emily's Business Venture

She had a steady job in marketing, but the Holy Spirit kept telling her to start her own business. She had always been very interested in organic skin care items and thought she could make a difference by giving people natural, eco-friendly options. She was scared to think about quitting her safe job, but the pull got stronger over time.

Emily decided to jump after much prayer and talk to her minister and friends for advice. She began her skincare line and promised to be honest and follow moral standards. She dedicated the business to God. During the first phase, which was hard because of money problems and competition in the market, Emily always looked to the Holy Spirit to help her make choices.

Her business grew faster than she thought it would over the next few years. People liked her story and how she cared about quality and the environment. Emily's business was successful not only because it made money but also because it helped people live healthier lives and buy food from local farms. She said that she was successful because the Holy Spirit led her, and she was ready to follow His lead even though it was scary.

These stories show how the Holy Spirit can help us progress in many areas of our lives, including work, health, relationships, and personal callings. Being open to His direction and ready to take risks in faith can make big changes in our lives and bring them more in line with God's plan.

Stepping Out in Faith with the Holy Spirit

In this chapter, you've learned how the Holy Spirit can guide, change, and improve every part of your life. It's clear that living fully with the Holy Spirit is not just a quiet experience but an active and changing relationship. In this friendship, you are being asked to live a life of faith, trust, and divine purpose. I want you to take the next step now.

Imagine what your life would be like if you let the Holy Spirit guide you all the time. Imagine how peaceful and clear your decisions will be, how your relationships will heal, and how fulfilling it will be to follow your God-given purpose. This is not a far-off dream; it is a real thing that awaits you if you have faith.

Trust in the Holy Spirit's Guidance

Trust the Holy Spirit in all of your choices, big and small. Make a promise to look to Him for direction every day. With an open heart, read the Bible and pray for knowledge. Then, listen for that still, small voice. Know that the Holy Spirit is with you and will guide your steps, so don't be afraid to go into the unknown.

Foster Your Relationship with the Holy Spirit

Grow your connection with the Holy Spirit by praying, worshiping, and thinking about God's word regularly. Set aside times during the day to be still and listen for His voice. Join your group of believers, tell them about your journey, and ask for help and advice. Remember that you are not alone. The Holy Spirit is with you all the time, and other Christians are there to walk with you.

Embrace Your Unique Purpose

Figure out what makes you special and how you can use those things to serve God and other people. Try new things and get out of your comfort zone. Trust that the Holy Spirit will lead you and give you the tools you need. Think about the things that have happened to you and how they can help you with your goal. Accept your calling with faith, knowing that the Holy Spirit gives you the power to do it.

A Life of Boldness and Faith

Be brave and have trust that doesn't waver. Follow the Holy Spirit's lead, even if it means taking chances and giving up things you want. Have faith that the Holy Spirit will guide and help you as you change jobs, fix broken relationships, or start a new mission. Show how living fully with the Holy Spirit can change people by the way you live.

Your Journey Continues

Remember that your journey with the Holy Spirit is still ongoing as you close this chapter and move on. Every step you take in faith will bring you new insights, chances, and gifts. Go on this journey with an open heart. You will find that living with the Holy Spirit makes your life full.

I want you to take a leap of faith today. Get help from the Holy Spirit, believe in your purpose, and live bravely for God's honor. A Spirit-filled life is an adventure that will help you grow, change, and find divine satisfaction. If you jump, the Holy Spirit will lead you to a life you could never have imagined.

Your purpose is the reason god wants to use you. The holy spirit is the only one who can determine which gifts you should have (1 Corinthians 12:11). Everyone who believes in Jesus will be able to drink from his river of living water and will never thirst again. God sent his spirit not only for you to gain his knowledge but also to ensure you have the wisdom to live in this world, for we are destroyed for lack of knowledge.

Chapter 5: Understanding the Gifts of the Spirit

The gifts of the holy spirit aren't just for ourselves but are meant to help the church and those around us. We'll break down each, showing how it can be used to make a positive impact. Understanding these gifts can transform your spiritual journey and empower you to live a life that glorifies God.

The Gift of Wisdom

The capacity to make wise decisions and assessments based on information and comprehension is the gift of wisdom. With the help of this gift, one can make decisions that are in line with God's will and perceive the world from His perspective. It entails not only knowing what is right but also putting that information to use in real-world situations. For example, a wise person may be able to effectively counsel others, providing insights that result in solutions that are consistent with God's will.

The Gift of Knowledge

The gift of knowledge involves understanding deep spiritual truths and mysteries. This gift allows a person to comprehend and explain biblical doctrines and principles clearly. It is often used in teaching and preaching, helping others to grasp the profound truths of Scripture. A person with this gift might have a strong desire to study the Bible and share their insights with others.

The Gift of Faith

A unique sort of faith that transcends ordinary belief is called faith—a firm and unwavering faith in God's ability and promises, regardless of the situation. Individuals possessing this talent motivate others with their steadfast faith in God. They strongly believe that God will supply and work miracles, which leads them to regularly take risky actions in ministry and life.

The Gift of Healing

The supernatural capacity to heal and rehabilitate patients is a component of the healing gift. This talent can become evident through acts of faith, like laying on hands or prayer. Healing might be spiritual, emotional, or bodily. People who possess this skill frequently have a deep empathy for the sick and a wish to see them healed.

The Gift of Miracles

The capacity to carry out deeds that reveal God's power and defy natural laws is known as the gift of miracles. This can involve unusual occurrences such as supernatural provision, healings, and other miracles. Individuals who possess this gift frequently feel a strong sense of God's presence and trust that He can work miracles.

The Gift of Prophecy

Messages from God are received and delivered by those with the gift of prophecy. This can involve making predictions, offering advice, or encouraging remarks. Prophets are frequently relied upon to convey God's truth to His people, assisting them in comprehending His plan and intentions. A strong sensitivity to the Holy Spirit and a dedication to telling the truth in love are prerequisites for this talent.

The Gift of Discernment

A person endowed with the gift of discernment is able to discriminate between good and wrong, truth and error, and the spirits responsible for different behaviors or teachings. This gift is essential to safeguarding the church against misleading doctrine and deceit. This ability allows one to perceive the influence and presence of spiritual entities, both good and evil, and to offer advice in accordance with those perceptions.

The Gift of Tongues

Speaking in a language that is foreign to the speaker—either heavenly or human—is known as the gift of tongues. This talent enables a person to have meaningful communication with God and is frequently used in prayer and worship. If understood in a congregational context, it can either be a warning to unbelievers or a tool for improvement.

The Gift of Interpretation of Tongues

The gift of tongues and the interpretation of tongues function together. This gift makes the message communicated in tongues understandable to others. It ensures that the message, beyond just the speaker's words, can uplift the entire church. To accurately communicate the meaning of the speech, one must be sensitive to the Holy Spirit.

The Gift of Helps

The capacity to aid others in practical ways—often behind the scenes—is known as the gift of assistance. This gift is essential to the church's efficient operation. Individuals possessing this talent are willing to go above and beyond to support the ministry, and they have a servant's heart. Serving others and participating in church activities brings them delight.

The Gift of Administration

The ability to effectively organize and manage tasks and resources is known as the gift of administration. Leadership positions in the church require this gift to plan and ensure everything goes as planned. Individuals with this talent are excellent managers and leaders because they have an eye for detail and a broad perspective.

Discovering your spiritual gifts can be a deeply enriching and empowering process. It allows you to understand how

God has uniquely equipped you to serve others and fulfill His purpose. Start with prayer, asking God to reveal the gifts He has placed within you. Spend time in quiet reflection, listening for His guidance. Pray specifically for wisdom and discernment, as James 1:5 encourages: "If any of you lacks wisdom, you should ask God, who gives generously to all without finding fault, and it will be given to you."

Reflect on your passions and interests. What activities make you feel most alive and fulfilled? What do you naturally excel at? Write down these observations. Consider times when you have felt particularly useful or satisfied in serving others. This can provide clues about your spiritual gifts. Assess your strengths and weaknesses honestly. Spiritual gifts often align with our natural strengths but are empowered by the Holy Spirit for greater impact. Acknowledge areas where you struggle, as these can sometimes indicate gifts you have yet to develop or understand fully.

Study passages in the Bible that discuss spiritual gifts, such as 1 Corinthians 12, Romans 12:6-8, and Ephesians 4:11-13. Reflect on each gift and consider how it might be manifested in your life. Journaling your thoughts and insights can help clarify your understanding and application. Look back at past experiences where you felt God's presence and empowerment in your actions. When have you felt that God was using you in a significant way? Consider the outcomes and impacts of these experiences. They can provide strong indicators of your spiritual gifts. Pay attention to what you desire to do and what brings you joy in serving others. Spiritual gifts often align with our God-given desires and passions. These activities may point to specific gifts if you find joy in teaching, encouraging, or helping others.

Ask friends, family, and members of your church who know you well to share their observations about your strengths and gifts. They may see patterns and abilities in you that you might overlook. Proverbs 15:22 says, "Plans fail for lack of counsel, but with many advisers, they succeed." Get involved in various church ministries and activities. This practical engagement can help you discover where you are most effective and fulfilled. Trying different roles allows you to experience firsthand how your gifts may be used in different contexts.

Find a mentor who can guide you in identifying and developing your spiritual gifts. A mentor can provide valuable insights, encouragement, and accountability. They can also help you navigate challenges and growth opportunities related to your gifts. Many churches offer spiritual gifts assessments or inventories. These tools can provide a structured way to explore your gifts. While not definitive, they can offer helpful insights and a starting point for further exploration.

Engage in activities and seek feedback on your performance. For example, if you feel led to teach, ask for constructive feedback after giving a lesson or leading a study. Positive feedback can confirm your gifts, while constructive criticism can guide you in honing them. Join a small group or Bible study where members can share their thoughts about each other's strengths and gifts. These discussions can provide a supportive environment for exploring and affirming spiritual gifts.

Identifying your spiritual gifts is a journey that combines self-reflection, practical engagement, and community feedback. Keep a journal of your reflections, experiences, and feedback from others. Over time, patterns will emerge that can help you identify your gifts more clearly. Once you have a sense of your spiritual gifts, seek opportunities to use them. Volunteer for roles that align with your gifts and be proactive in serving others. The more you use your gifts, the more they will develop and become evident. Continue to pray for God's guidance and confirmation of your gifts. Ask the Holy Spirit to help you grow and use your gifts effectively for His glory. By combining reflective exercises with feedback from your community, you can gain a clearer understanding of your spiritual gifts. Embrace this journey with an open heart, and you will find greater fulfillment and purpose in your walk with God.

Developing and strengthening your spiritual gifts requires practice, dedication, and a heart willing to grow and serve. Here are practical steps to help you nurture and enhance your spiritual gifts effectively.

First, embrace a mindset of continuous learning. Just as with any skill, spiritual gifts can be honed and refined over time. Approach your gifts with humility and a willingness to learn. Study relevant scriptures, attend workshops or seminars, and read books by respected Christian authors to gain deeper insights into your specific gifts. The Bible provides a wealth of knowledge and examples of spiritual gifts in action. Regularly reading and meditating on passages such as 1 Corinthians 12, Romans 12:6-8, and Ephesians 4:11-13 will help you understand how these gifts operate within the body of Christ and how you can apply them in your own life.

Practice is essential for growth. Actively seek opportunities to use your gifts in various settings. If you have the gift of teaching, volunteer to lead a Bible study or Sunday school class. If your gift is hospitality, open your home for fellowship gatherings or support church events that involve welcoming newcomers. The more you use your gifts, the more comfortable and proficient you will become. It's important to remember that practice doesn't mean perfection; it means progress. Each time you use your gift, you learn something new and become more effective.

Engage in regular self-reflection and evaluation. After using your gifts, take time to reflect on the experience. What went well? What could be improved? How did others respond? Self-reflection allows you to identify areas for growth and to celebrate your progress. Keep a journal to document your experiences, insights, and the feedback you receive from others. This will help you track your development over time and see how God is working through you.

Seek feedback from trusted mentors and peers. Honest and constructive feedback is invaluable for growth. Ask people you trust to observe you and provide feedback on how you are using your gifts. Their insights can offer new perspectives and highlight areas you might not have considered. Be open to criticism and willing to make adjustments based on the feedback you receive. Remember, the goal is to grow and improve, not to be perfect.

Dedicate time for prayer and seeking God's guidance. Prayer is essential in developing your spiritual gifts. Regularly ask God for wisdom, strength, and opportunities to use your gifts. Seek His direction in how best to serve others and grow in your gifting. Listen for the Holy Spirit's promptings and be obedient to His guidance. God is the giver of spiritual gifts, and He desires to help you develop them for His glory and the edification of the church.

Connect with a community of believers. Being part of a supportive church community can greatly enhance your growth. Surround yourself with people who encourage and challenge you to use your gifts. Participate in small groups, prayer meetings, and ministry teams where you can practice your gifts and receive support from others. The body of Christ is designed to function together, with each member contributing their unique gifts for the common good. By staying connected, you can learn from others and grow in a supportive environment.

Stay humble and teachable. Spiritual gifts are not a measure of your worth or status but tools for serving others.

Always maintain an attitude of humility and gratitude. Recognize that your gifts come from God and are meant to glorify Him, not yourself. Be willing to learn from others and to grow in areas where you may feel weak or inexperienced.

Set specific goals for your growth. Identify areas where you want to improve and set achievable goals to help you get there. For example, if you want to grow in the gift of teaching, set a goal to prepare and deliver a certain number of lessons within a given timeframe. If you have the gift of encouragement, set a goal to reach out to a certain number of people each week. Setting goals helps you stay focused and motivated in your development.

Cultivate a lifestyle of service. Your spiritual gifts are most effectively developed and strengthened when used in the service of others. Look for ways to serve within your church, community, and beyond. As you serve, you will not only bless others but also grow in your gifts. Serving helps you step out of your comfort zone, face new challenges, and rely more on God's strength and guidance.

Using your spiritual gifts to serve others is a foundational principle in the Christian faith, deeply rooted in the teachings of the Bible. It brings not only fulfillment and purpose to your life but also contributes significantly to the well-being and growth of the church community and beyond. Here's an exploration of why serving others with your gifts is so crucial and how it leads to a more meaningful and purposeful existence.

The Bible teaches that every believer has been endowed with unique spiritual gifts by the Holy Spirit. These gifts are not given for personal glory or selfish gain but are meant to benefit others and build up the body of Christ. In 1 Peter 4:10, we read, "Each of you should use whatever gift you have received to serve others as faithful stewards of God's grace in its various forms." This passage underscores the responsibility and privilege of using our gifts to serve others, highlighting that we are stewards of God's manifold grace.

Serving others with your spiritual gifts brings a profound sense of fulfillment. When you use your gifts in service, you align yourself with God's purpose for your life. This alignment creates a deep sense of satisfaction and joy because you are functioning in the way God designed you. For instance, someone with the gift of teaching will find great joy in helping others understand biblical truths. In contrast, someone with the gift of hospitality will experience fulfillment in creating welcoming environments for others.

Serving with your gifts allows you to see the impact you have on others, which is incredibly rewarding. Seeing someone grow in their faith, find encouragement, or receive help because of your service can bring a deep sense of purpose and accomplishment. This positive impact reinforces the value of your contributions and motivates you to continue serving.

Using your gifts to serve others also fosters a sense of community and belonging. When everyone uses their gifts, the church becomes a vibrant, dynamic body where each member plays a crucial role. This mutual dependency and cooperation create strong bonds among believers. As Paul writes in 1 Corinthians 12:12-27, the church is like a body with many parts, each part essential and interdependent. Serving others helps you connect with people, build relationships, and foster a supportive and loving community.

It challenges you to step out of your comfort zone, rely on God's strength, and develop new skills. As you serve, you often encounter situations that stretch your faith and character, leading to personal growth and deeper reliance on God. This growth not only benefits you but also enhances your ability to serve others more effectively.

Another significant aspect of using your gifts to serve others is that they bring glory to God. When you serve in a way that reflects Christ's love and humility, you point others to Him. Your service becomes a testimony of God's grace and power at work in your life. As Jesus said in Matthew 5:16, "Let your light shine before others, that they may see your good deeds and glorify your Father in heaven." Serving others with your gifts is a tangible way to express your faith and demonstrate God's love to the world.

Serving others also combats selfishness and fosters humility. It shifts your focus from your own needs and desires to the needs of others. This outward focus helps you develop a Christ-like attitude of humility and compassion. Philippians 2:3-4 encourages us, "Do nothing out of selfish ambition or vain conceit. Rather, in humility, value others above yourselves, not looking to your own interests but each of you to the interests of the others." By serving others, you cultivate a heart of humility and selflessness.

Using your gifts to serve others creates a ripple effect of positive influence. When you serve others, you inspire them to use their gifts as well. Your example can motivate others to step into their God-given roles, creating a culture of service within the community. This collective effort amplifies the impact, leading to greater unity and effectiveness in fulfilling the church's mission.

Serving others with your gifts also brings eternal rewards. While the immediate benefits of service are fulfilling, the Bible promises that God rewards faithful service. In Matthew 25:21, Jesus says, "Well done, good and faithful servant! You have been faithful with a few things; I will put you in charge of many things.

Come and share your master's happiness!" This assurance of eternal reward gives additional meaning and purpose to your service, knowing that it pleases God and has lasting significance.

Using your spiritual gifts to serve others is a vital aspect of the Christian life. It brings fulfillment and purpose by aligning you with God's design, fostering community, promoting spiritual growth, glorifying God, cultivating humility, inspiring others, and earning eternal rewards.

Embrace your gifts and commit to using them in service, and you will experience the profound joy and purpose that come from making a meaningful difference in the lives of others.

Real-Life Examples of Using Spiritual Gifts to Make a Difference

Real-life stories of individuals using their spiritual gifts to serve others provide powerful inspiration and illustrate the profound impact these gifts can have on communities. Here are some inspiring examples of people using their spiritual gifts to make a difference:

Example 1: The Gift of Teaching - Dr. Tony Evans

Dr. Tony Evans is a well-known pastor, author, and speaker who has profoundly impacted the Christian community with his gift of teaching. Through his clear and engaging biblical teaching, he has helped countless individuals understand and apply the Word of God to their lives.

Dr. Evans founded The Urban Alternative, a ministry dedicated to restoring hope and transforming lives through the teaching of God's Word. His sermons, books, and radio broadcasts reach millions, providing sound biblical teaching that empowers believers to live out their faith.

Dr. Evans' commitment to using his gift of teaching has educated and inspired individuals and fostered spiritual growth within communities. His work demonstrates how the gift of teaching can illuminate truth, build faith, and encourage a deeper relationship with God.

Example 2: The Gift of Hospitality - Mary and Martha House

The Mary and Martha House, a shelter for homeless women and children in Tampa, Florida, exemplifies the gift of hospitality in action. Founded by a group of women who saw a need in their community, the shelter provides a safe and welcoming environment for those in crisis. The founders and volunteers use their gift of hospitality to create a warm, supportive atmosphere where residents can heal and rebuild their lives.

The Mary and Martha House offers shelter and a range of services, including counseling, job training, and life skills education. Using their hospitality gift, the volunteers provide a nurturing environment that helps residents regain their dignity and hope. Their work shows how hospitality can be a powerful tool for ministry, offering comfort and support to those in need.

Example 3: The Gift of Mercy - Mother Teresa

Mother Teresa, known for her extraordinary compassion and mercy, dedicated her life to serving the poorest of the poor. With the gift of mercy, she founded the Missionaries of Charity, an order that serves the needy, sick, and dying worldwide. Her deep empathy for the suffering and her relentless commitment to helping those in need exemplify the gift of mercy.

Mother Teresa's work in the slums of Calcutta brought hope and dignity to the marginalized. Her ministry provided not only physical care but also emotional and spiritual support. Using her gift of mercy, Mother Teresa impacted countless lives and inspired others to serve with compassion and love.

Example 4: The Gift of Administration - Nehemiah

In the Bible, Nehemiah is a prime example of someone using the gift of administration to make a significant difference. When he learned about the broken walls of Jerusalem, he felt called to rebuild them. With exceptional organizational skills and strategic planning, Nehemiah rallied the people, secured resources, and overcame opposition to complete the project.

Nehemiah's leadership and administrative abilities restored not only the physical walls but also the people's morale and faith. His story highlights how the gift of administration can be instrumental in achieving God's purposes and bringing about community transformation.

Example 5: The Gift of Giving - Truett Cathy

Truett Cathy, the founder of Chick-fil-A, used his gift of giving to impact his community and beyond significantly. Known for his generosity, Cathy established numerous charitable initiatives, including scholarships, foster homes, and camps for underprivileged children. His commitment to giving extended to his business practices, where he emphasized caring for employees and customers alike.

Through his philanthropic efforts, Cathy demonstrated how the gift of giving can be a powerful force for good. His contributions have provided education, support, and opportunities for countless individuals, reflecting the transformative power of generosity.

Example 6: The Gift of Healing - Heidi Baker

Heidi Baker, co-founder of Iris Global, has used her gift of healing to bring hope and restoration to the poor and needy in Mozambique. Through her ministry, she has witnessed countless physical and spiritual miraculous healings. Her work includes healing, feeding programs, orphan care, and community development. Baker's dedication to using her gift of healing has brought tangible change to communities, transforming lives and demonstrating God's love in action. Her ministry shows how the gift of healing can address immediate needs and foster long-term spiritual and physical well-being.

Example 7: The Gift of Leadership - Martin Luther King Jr.

Martin Luther King Jr. is an exemplary figure who used his leadership gift to spearhead the civil rights movement in the United States. With courage, vision, and a deep sense of justice, he led peaceful protests and advocated for the end of racial segregation and discrimination.

King's leadership inspired a movement that brought about significant legal and social changes, promoting equality and justice. His ability to mobilize and inspire others demonstrates how the gift of leadership can bring about profound societal transformation.

These real-life examples illustrate the diverse ways spiritual gifts can be used to serve others and make a meaningful impact. Whether through teaching, hospitality, mercy, administration, giving, healing, or leadership, each gift plays a crucial role in building the community and advancing God's kingdom. By following these examples, we can be inspired to discover and use our gifts to serve others, bringing fulfillment and purpose to our lives and glory to God.

Each spiritual gift holds unique value, contributing to the overall health and vitality of the church and community. By appreciating and utilizing these gifts, believers can fulfill their God-given purposes and encourage others to do the same. Understanding the distinctive contributions of each gift fosters unity and collaboration within the body of Christ. Here, we explore the unique value of various spiritual gifts and encourage readers to appreciate their and others' spiritual talents.

The Gift of Teaching: Teaching is invaluable for imparting knowledge and understanding God's Word. Teachers help others grasp complex biblical truths and apply them to their lives. They provide clarity and insight, fostering spiritual growth and maturity within the community. By appreciating this gift, we acknowledge the importance of sound doctrine and the need for continual learning and growth in faith.

The Gift of Hospitality: Hospitality is a gift that creates a welcoming and inclusive environment. Those with this gift make others feel valued and cared for, often providing a sense of belonging and comfort. Hospitality extends beyond mere entertainment; it involves genuine care and compassion for others. Recognizing the value of hospitality helps us see the importance of creating spaces where people feel safe, loved, and accepted.

The Gift of Mercy: The gift of mercy is characterized by deep compassion and empathy for those suffering. Individuals with this gift are often drawn to help the sick, the poor, and the marginalized. Their actions reflect the heart of Christ, bringing comfort and hope to those in need. By valuing the gift of mercy, we emphasize the importance of compassion and the transformative power of love in action.

The Gift of Administration: The gift of administration involves organizing, planning, and managing tasks efficiently. Administrators ensure that the various activities and ministries within the church run smoothly. Their ability to coordinate efforts and manage resources is crucial for effective ministry. Appreciating this gift highlights the need for order and structure, enabling other gifts to flourish in a well-organized environment.

The Gift of Giving: The gift of giving goes beyond financial contributions and includes the generous sharing of time, talents, and resources. Givers often have a heart for supporting others and advancing God's work. Their generosity enables various ministries to thrive and meet community needs. By valuing the gift of giving, we recognize the impact of generosity and the blessings it brings to both the giver and receiver.

The Gift of Healing: Healing manifests in restoring health and wholeness through prayer and faith. Those with this gift often see miraculous recoveries and provide spiritual, emotional, and physical healing. Appreciating the gift of healing underscores the power of God's intervention and the importance of faith in the healing process.

The Gift of Leadership: Leadership is a gift that inspires and guides others toward a common goal. Leaders provide vision, direction, and motivation, helping the community to achieve its mission. Their influence can bring about significant change and progress. By valuing the gift of leadership, we recognize the necessity of strong, visionary guidance in achieving collective goals.

The Gift of Prophecy: The gift of prophecy involves receiving and delivering messages from God. Prophets often provide guidance, encouragement, and correction, helping the community stay aligned with God's will. This gift brings clarity and direction, usually calling people back to God's truths. Appreciating the gift of prophecy highlights the importance of divine revelation and spiritual insight.

The Gift of Encouragement: Encouragement is a gift that uplifts and motivates others. Encouragers provide support and affirmation, helping people to persevere through challenges. Their words and actions inspire hope and confidence. By valuing the gift of encouragement, we emphasize the importance of building each other up and fostering a positive, supportive environment.

The Gift of Faith: The gift of faith involves a solid and unwavering trust in God's promises and power. Those with this gift inspire others with their confident reliance on God, especially under challenging circumstances. Their faith often leads to miraculous outcomes and bold actions. Appreciating the gift of faith underscores the importance of trust and dependence on God in every aspect of life. The Gift of Helps: The gift of help is characterized by a willingness to assist others in practical ways. Helpers often work behind the scenes, ensuring that needs are met and tasks are completed.

Their contributions are essential for the smooth functioning of the community. By valuing the gift of help, we recognize the significance of service and the impact of faithful, humble work. Each spiritual gift is uniquely valuable, contributing to the diverse and vibrant life of the church. By appreciating our gifts and those of others, we foster a spirit of unity and cooperation.

Recognizing the importance of each gift helps us see each person's integral role in God's plan. Embrace your spiritual gifts with gratitude and use them to serve others, bringing fulfillment and purpose to your life and glory to God. Encourage others to do the same, creating a community where every gift is valued and everyone is empowered to contribute.

Praying In the Spirit

When praying in tongues, you're doing something beneficial, but it must have the understanding if you're in a public setting.

1 Corinthians 14-15

When you pray in tongues, it illuminates your mind, stirs up emotions, and connects you to whomever you're praying for. God will give you the interpretation of what you were praying when you asked. Praying in the spirit and praying with understanding is vital to us and God. We have counsel from Proverbs 20:5 (A plan in a man's heart is like water in a deep well, but a man of understanding draws it out). Whenever you start meditating on the goodness of God, the spirit will let you see God's heart and his love for you. When you pray in tongues, you are interceding for another region or a person who is not around you at the time.

God's grace

God's grace is his power. When you acknowledge your weakness, he will give you his power. God will give you the Holy Spirit when he knows He can count on you. No, you don't need to be perfect because only one is perfect in this World, and that is Jesus Christ. A person who speaks in tongues strengthens him or herself; the enemy doesn't want you strong because they think the stronger you are in the spirit, you will be as strong for Christ, and then you will be a threat to Satan's Kingdom.

Chapter 6: Overcoming Challenges with the Holy Spirit

Temptation and peer pressure are common problems that can hinder our spiritual journey if we don't deal with them wisely and strongly. The power of the Holy Spirit is a useful and effective way to get through these tough times. With the help and direction of the Holy Spirit, here are some ways to deal with temptation and peer pressure.

1. Understand Your Identity in Christ:

The first step in overcoming peer pressure and temptation is understanding who you are in Christ. Accepting Jesus as your Savior makes you a new creation (2 Corinthians 5:17). This new identity should shape your decisions and actions. Remembering that you are a child of God, empowered by the Holy Spirit, can give you the strength to resist negative influences and make choices that align with your faith.

2. Stay Rooted in the Word of God:

The Bible is a powerful tool in resisting temptation and peer pressure. Psalm 119:11 says, "I have hidden your word in my heart that I might not sin against you." Regularly reading and meditating on Scripture helps you internalize God's truths, which can guide you when faced with difficult situations. Verses that remind you of God's promises and your commitment to Him can provide the strength needed to stand firm.

3. Pray for Strength and Guidance:

Prayer is a direct line to the Holy Spirit, who is always ready to assist you. When you feel tempted or pressured, pray for strength and guidance. Philippians 4:6-7 encourages us to present our requests to God, promising that His peace will guard our hearts and minds. Asking the Holy Spirit for help in moments of weakness invites His power into your situation, giving you the courage to make the right choices.

4. Surround Yourself with Supportive People:

The company you keep significantly influences your ability to resist peer pressure. Proverbs 13:20 advises, "Walk with the wise and become wise, for a companion of fools suffers harm." Surrounding yourself with fellow believers who support your faith journey can provide encouragement and accountability. These individuals can pray with you, offer godly advice, and help you stay focused on your spiritual goals.

5. Practice Self-Control:

Self-control is a fruit of the Spirit (Galatians 5:22-23) and a crucial aspect of resisting temptation. By relying on the Holy Spirit, you can develop and strengthen this quality. Practicing self-control involves making deliberate choices that reflect your commitment to Christ. It means saying no to harmful behaviors and yes to actions that honor God. The Holy Spirit empowers you to exercise self-control, even in challenging situations.

6. Use Scripture to Combat Lies:

Temptation often comes in the form of lies and deceit. The devil may convince you that giving in to peer pressure or temptation is harmless or beneficial. Combat these lies with the truth of Scripture. When Jesus was tempted in the wilderness, He responded with God's Word (Matthew 4:1-11). Similarly, you can use specific Bible verses to counteract the lies and reinforce your resolve to stay true to your faith.

7. Reflect on the Consequences:

Consider the long-term consequences of giving in to peer pressure or temptation. James 1:14-15 warns that temptation, when conceived, gives birth to sin, which leads to death. Reflecting on the potential spiritual, emotional, and relational damage can deter you from making choices that are contrary to God's will. The Holy Spirit can help you see the bigger picture and understand the impact of your actions.

8. Develop a Plan of Action:

Making a plan ahead of time can help you handle scenarios where you may feel tempted or pressured by other people. There should be ways to avoid scenarios that could be dangerous, set limits, and be ready with answers when pressured into this plan. The Holy Spirit can help you make and carry out this plan by giving insight and knowledge to safeguard your spiritual health.

9. Confess and Seek Forgiveness:

When you fall into temptation or succumb to peer pressure, it's essential to confess your sins and seek forgiveness. 1 John 1:9 assures us that if we confess our sins, God is faithful and just to forgive us and purify us from all unrighteousness. The Holy Spirit convicts us of our sins, leading us to repentance and helping us restore our relationship with God.

10. Keep Your Focus on Jesus:

Ultimately, keeping your focus on Jesus is the key to overcoming peer pressure and temptation. Hebrews 12:2 encourages us to fix our eyes on Jesus, the author and perfecter of our faith. By maintaining a close relationship with Him, you can draw strength and inspiration to live a life that honors God. The Holy Spirit helps you keep your focus on Jesus, reminding you of His love, sacrifice, and the eternal rewards that await those who remain faithful.

Ways to Find Inner Strength During Tough Times, Focusing on Building a Strong Connection with the Holy Spirit

1. Cultivate a Habit of Daily Prayer:

Prayer is the foundation of a strong connection with the Holy Spirit. It opens a direct line of communication with God, allowing you to express your fears, hopes, and needs. During tough times, consistent prayer can provide a sense of peace and clarity. Philippians 4:6-7 encourages us to present our requests to God through prayer and thanksgiving, promising that His peace will guard our hearts and minds. Establishing a daily prayer routine helps you stay connected to the Holy Spirit, drawing on His strength and guidance.

2. Immerse Yourself in Scripture:

The Bible is a source of comfort and strength, filled with God's promises and examples of His faithfulness. Regularly reading and meditating on Scripture helps internalize these truths, providing a solid foundation to stand on during tough times. Verses like Isaiah 40:31 remind us that those who hope in the Lord will renew their strength. By immersing yourself in God's Word, you allow the Holy Spirit to speak to you, offering wisdom and encouragement when you need it most.

3. Practice Listening Prayer:

Listening to prayer involves not just speaking to God but also being still and listening for His voice. Psalm 46:10 urges us to "be still, and know that I am God." This practice helps you become more attuned to the Holy Spirit's gentle promptings. Find a quiet place, free from distractions, where you can sit in silence and open your heart to the Holy Spirit. Journaling your thoughts and any impressions you receive can help you discern His guidance and experience His comforting presence.

4. Engage in Worship:

Worship is a powerful way to connect with the Holy Spirit and draw strength. It shifts your focus from your problems to God's greatness and faithfulness. Worship can take many forms, from singing hymns and contemporary worship songs to expressing gratitude and praise. Acts 16:25-26 describes how Paul and Silas, imprisoned and facing hardship, sang hymns and prayed, leading to a miraculous release. Worship invites the Holy Spirit into your situation, transforming despair into hope and strength.

5. Seek Community Support:

God designed us for community, and the support of fellow believers can be invaluable during tough times. Hebrews 10:24-25 encourages us to spur one another on toward love and good deeds and not to give up meeting together. Being part of a church, small group, or prayer circle provides a network of people who can pray with you, offer encouragement, and share their own experiences of the Holy Spirit's strength. Their support can bolster your faith and remind you that you are not alone.

6. Reflect on God's Faithfulness:

Reflecting on past experiences where you have seen God's faithfulness can reinforce your trust in His strength. Keeping a journal of answered prayers, significant moments of guidance, and times when the Holy Spirit has provided comfort can serve as a powerful reminder during tough times. Psalm 77:11-12 speaks of recalling the Lord's deeds and meditating on His works. This practice helps you see the continuity of God's presence in your life, providing confidence that He will continue to sustain you.

7. Embrace the Fruits of the Spirit:

The fruits of the Spirit—love, joy, peace, patience, kindness, goodness, faithfulness, gentleness, and self-control (Galatians 5:22-23)—are manifestations of the Holy Spirit's work in your life. Cultivating these attributes can help you maintain a positive and resilient mindset. For example, practicing patience can help you endure hardships while fostering peace can reduce anxiety and provide clarity. The Holy Spirit empowers you to develop these traits, equipping you with inner strength.

8. Trust in God's Plan:

Trusting that God has a plan for your life, even when you cannot see it, can provide immense strength. Proverbs 3:5- 6 advises us to trust in the Lord with all our heart and lean not on our understanding. Trusting in God's sovereignty helps you surrender your fears and uncertainties to Him. The Holy Spirit reassures you of God's perfect timing and purposes, helping you find peace amid chaos.

9. Practice Gratitude:

Gratitude shifts your focus from what you lack to what you have, fostering a positive outlook. 1 Thessalonians 5:18

encourages us to give thanks in all circumstances. Regularly expressing gratitude opens your heart to the Holy Spirit's joy and peace, which can fortify you during tough times. Keep a gratitude journal or make it a habit to thank God for His blessings, big and small, each day.

10. Engage in Acts of Service:

Serving others, even when you are struggling, can be a source of strength and encouragement. Acts 20:35 reminds us that it is more blessed to give than to receive. Helping those in need shifts your focus from your problems and allows the Holy Spirit to work through you to bless others. This act of selflessness can renew your spirit and provide a sense of purpose and fulfillment.

The Holy Spirit is often described as a Comforter and Counselor, offering us solace and encouragement in our daily lives. This divine presence works in subtle yet profound ways, providing strength, peace, and guidance. Here are some relatable examples of how the Holy Spirit provides comfort and encouragement in everyday life.

1. During Moments of Personal Loss:

Consider Sarah, who recently lost her grandmother. Her grandmother was a pillar of strength in her life, and Sarah felt an overwhelming sense of loss and grief. One evening, while sitting quietly in her room, she decided to pray. As she poured out her heart, she felt a warm, comforting presence envelop her. This was the Holy Spirit providing reassurance and reminding her of the eternal life promised to believers. This experience gave Sarah the peace she needed to cope with her grief and the strength to move forward.

2. Facing Career Challenges:

David was at a crossroads in his career, struggling to decide whether to stay in his current job or pursue a new opportunity that seemed risky. He felt stressed and unsure. One morning, during his prayer time, he asked the Holy Spirit for guidance. Later that day, he felt an inexplicable sense of calm and clarity about pursuing the new opportunity. This inner peace was a sign from the Holy Spirit, providing David with the courage and assurance to take the leap of faith. His decision, guided by the Holy Spirit, led to a fulfilling and successful career path.

3. Overcoming Daily Anxiety:

Emily often struggled with anxiety, especially about her future. Simple tasks sometimes felt overwhelming, and she frequently worried about things beyond her control. One day, while reading her Bible, she came across Philippians 4:6-7, which encourages believers to present their requests to God with thanksgiving and promises that His peace will guard their hearts and minds. Emily decided to implement this advice, praying daily and giving thanks for the positives in her life. Over time, she noticed a significant reduction in her anxiety, feeling a deep sense of peace and reassurance. The Holy Spirit had been working in her heart, providing the comfort and encouragement she needed to confidently face each day.

4. Navigating Relationship Conflicts:

Mark and his brother hadn't talked to each other in years because of a mistake that turned into a big fight. One Sunday, Mark got a big push while listening to a sermon about forgiving others. He knew this push was from the Holy Spirit telling him to make peace with his brother. Even though he was scared, Mark reached out, and they agreed to meet. They were honest and humble in their talk, which led to forgiveness and a new start in their relationship. Mark had the confidence to take the first step and the peace of mind from knowing peace was possible because of the Holy Spirit.

5. Seeking Direction in Parenting:

Jessica, who had two kids, often felt like she couldn't handle all the hurdles of raising her kids. She had trouble finding the right mix between love and discipline and was unsure if she was making the right choices. During her quiet time one night, she prayed for knowledge and direction. The following day, she felt very calm and had a clear idea for a new way to deal with her kids' bedtime routine, which had been a big source of stress. Their evenings became more organized and peaceful when they started using this new plan. Jessica knew that the Holy Spirit had led her and given her comfort and valuable ways to deal with her problems as a mom.

6. Encouragement in Times of Loneliness:

Tom had just moved for work and felt alone since his family and friends were no longer close. He joined a church in the area, but he still felt alone. He begged for company and support one night when he was feeling down. Soon after, he got a call from a coworker asking him to a meeting with a small group. Going to this group not only helped him make new friends but also made him feel like he was part of a community. Tom felt better because he knew the Holy Spirit had heard his prayer and had put him in touch with people who could help him.

7. Inspiration for Creative Projects:

Samantha, a writer, often got stuck and couldn't think of what to write next. She prayed for inspiration and direction because she was upset. She had a new idea that made her happy when she woke up the following day. She got a lot of ideas and focus, which made it easy and fun for her to write. She realized this success was the Holy Spirit's answer to her prayer, inspiring her to be creative.

8. Comfort During Illness:

Carlos was told he had a dangerous illness, which made him scared and unsure of what would happen next. Even though his family and friends were there for him, he often felt alone in his battle. He prayed for relief and strength one night. He felt a deep peace and knew he wasn't fighting this battle alone as he prayed. Carlos faced his treatment with hope and strength because of this comfort from the Holy Spirit. He found strength in small wins along the way.

9. Guidance in Financial Decisions:

Laura had to make a big choice about money that could affect her family's future. Her sense of duty and fear of making a bad choice were heavy. She prayed to get wise and discover her way. Soon after, she felt a strong urge to talk to a financial adviser and make a choice she had been on the fence about. By following this advice, her family was able to get ahead financially and grow. Laura knew the Holy Spirit had given her the knowledge to pick the right path.

It would be best to build resilience to handle life's trials with strength and grace. A holistic way to deal with problems is to combine spiritual routines with useful life skills. These steps, including spiritual and physical parts, will help you become more resilient through your faith.

Start by making prayer a regular part of your life. You should set aside time daily to pray, like in the morning, during breaks, or before bed. Every day, prayer helps you connect with God and gives you strength and happiness. Keeping a prayer book where you can write down your prayers, thoughts, and reflections can be helpful. This will help you see how God answers your prayers over time.

Focusing on breathing and being in the present moment can help you be less stressed and more emotionally stable. Add mindfulness methods to your prayer time.

Reading the Bible regularly is very important. Stick to a structured Bible reading plan to ensure you read God's Word daily. It will give you daily knowledge and comfort. Remember important verses that speak to you. Having these verses in your heart can help you feel better right away when things are hard.

When you read the Bible, use critical thinking skills and think about how the lessons can be applied to problems in the current world and your own life.

Building a group that helps each other is another important step. Take part in small groups, Bible study groups, and church events. These groups offer help, motivation, and responsibility. Connect with people who will pray with you and help you through prayer and mutual support. Making and keeping a network of helpful friends and family is also essential. Strong social ties can give you emotional support and practical help when you need it.

Practicing thanks can make you much more resilient. As you pray, remember to be thankful and thank God for all the good things He has done for you, even when things are hard. Writing down daily blessings and things you are grateful for in a gratitude book can help you focus on the good things in your life instead of the bad, making you feel better.

Developing a positive mindset is vital. Regularly affirm your faith and God's promises, reminding yourself of His goodness and faithfulness. Replace negative thoughts with positive affirmations grounded in Scripture. For example, when feeling overwhelmed, remind yourself of Philippians

4:13, "I can do all things through Christ who strengthens me." Positive self-talk can improve mental resilience and help you maintain a hopeful attitude.

Incorporating physical self-care is also essential. Exercise regularly, eat a balanced diet, and ensure you get enough sleep. Physical health impacts mental and emotional well-being, which is critical for resilience. View your body as a temple of the Holy Spirit (1 Corinthians 6:19-20), and take care of it accordingly. Engage in relaxing and rejuvenating activities, such as taking walks, practicing yoga, or enjoying a hobby. These activities can reduce stress and increase overall well-being.

Another effective strategy is setting realistic goals and taking actionable steps toward them. Break down larger goals into manageable tasks and celebrate small victories along the way. This approach can prevent overwhelming feelings and build confidence in overcoming challenges. Trust in God's plan for your life (Jeremiah 29:11) and seek His guidance in setting and achieving your goals.

Having a sense of purpose can make you much more resilient. Think about your life's meaning and how it fits God's calling. Doing things that matter and helping other people can give you a sense of fulfillment and perspective. Help out at church or in the community, be a guide to someone, or help a neighbor who needs it. Volunteering not only helps other people but also improves your life and makes you feel more connected to God's work.

Learning to manage stress effectively is crucial for resilience. Identify stressors in your life and develop coping strategies. Practice deep breathing exercises, meditation, or other relaxation techniques to calm your mind. Turning to Scripture for encouragement and comfort can also be helpful. Verses like Psalm 46:10, "Be still, and know that I am God," remind you to find peace in God's presence.

Embrace the power of forgiveness. Holding onto grudges and resentment can weigh heavily on your spirit. Follow the biblical principle of forgiveness, as taught in Ephesians 4:32, "Be kind and compassionate to one another, forgiving each other, just as in Christ God forgave you." Letting go of past hurts frees you to move forward with a lighter heart and a more resilient spirit.

By integrating these spiritual practices and practical life skills, you can build resilience through faith. This holistic approach not only strengthens your connection with God but also equips you to face life's challenges with confidence and grace.

Personal Stories of Overcoming Adversity with the Holy Spirit's Help

Adversity is an inevitable part of life, but through the power and guidance of the Holy Spirit, we can overcome even the most daunting challenges. Here are some inspiring personal stories of individuals who have triumphed over adversity with the Holy Spirit's help, offering hope and inspiration for leaders.

1. Sarah's Journey through Grief:

Sarah had always been close to her grandmother, who was not only a family matriarch but also her spiritual mentor. When her grandmother passed away, Sarah was devastated. She felt a deep void and struggled to find comfort. One night, overwhelmed with grief, Sarah knelt in prayer, asking the Holy Spirit for comfort. As she prayed, she felt a warm, reassuring presence. The Holy Spirit brought to mind scriptures her grandmother used to share, particularly Psalm 34:18, "The Lord is close to the brokenhearted and saves those who are crushed in spirit." This verse resonated deeply with Sarah, and she felt an unexplainable peace wash over her. Over the next few months, Sarah continued to lean on the Holy Spirit through prayer and reading the Bible. She found solace in her church community and gradually healed. Today, Sarah leads a grief support group at her church, helping others find comfort and strength in their faith during difficult times.

2. David's Career Crisis:

David was at a critical juncture in his career, facing a significant decision that would impact his future. His current job was stable but unfulfilling, while a new opportunity promised growth but came with substantial risks. Feeling anxious and unsure, David turned to prayer, seeking the Holy Spirit's guidance. One morning, during his quiet time, he felt an overwhelming sense of peace about taking the new opportunity. He recalled the words of Proverbs 3:5- 6, "Trust in the Lord with all your heart and lean not on your understanding; in all your ways submit to him, and he will make your paths straight." Encouraged by this clarity, David took the leap of faith. The new role, while challenging, turned out to be incredibly rewarding. David excelled, finding new purpose and satisfaction in his work. He often shares his story with his team, encouraging them to seek divine guidance in their professional lives.

3. Emily's Battle with Anxiety:

Emily had struggled with anxiety for years. The constant worry about the future and fear of failure had become overwhelming. One Sunday, during a sermon on Philippians 4:6-7, "Do not be anxious about anything, but in every situation, by prayer and petition, with thanksgiving, present your requests to God. And the peace of God, which transcends all understanding, will guard your hearts and your minds in Christ Jesus," Emily felt a spark of hope. She decided to apply this scripture to her life, dedicating time each day to pray and give thanks, even for the smallest blessings. Gradually, she noticed a change. The Holy Spirit provided her with a sense of calm and reassurance. She joined a support group at her church, where she met others dealing with similar issues. Through prayer, community, and focusing on God's promises, Emily's anxiety diminished. Today, she is a mental health advocate, sharing her journey and encouraging others to seek the Holy Spirit's peace.

4. Mark's Family Reconciliation:

Mark and his brother had been estranged for over a decade due to a severe misunderstanding. The bitterness and pride had built a wall between them. One evening, after a powerful sermon on forgiveness, Mark felt the Holy Spirit nudging him to reach out to his brother. Ephesians 4:32 echoed in his mind, "Be kind and compassionate to one another, forgiving each other, just as in Christ God forgave you." Despite his fears, Mark made the call. To his surprise, his brother was receptive. They met, shared their grievances, and, through heartfelt conversations and prayer, forgave each other. The Holy Spirit had softened their hearts, leading to reconciliation. This renewed relationship became a testament to the power of forgiveness. Mark now mentors young men in his community, teaching them the importance of forgiveness and reconciliation.

5. Jessica's Parenting Challenges:

Jessica, a mother of two, often felt overwhelmed by the demands of parenting. Her youngest child had special needs, requiring constant attention and care. She frequently felt inadequate and exhausted. One night, she cried out to the Holy Spirit for help. The next morning, she felt prompted to read Isaiah 40:29-31, "He gives strength to the weary and increases the power of the weak. Even youths grow tired and weary, and young men stumble and fall, but those who hope in the Lord will renew their strength. They will soar on wings like eagles; they will run and not grow weary; they will walk and not be faint." These verses gave her renewed hope. She sought support from her church's parenting group, where she found practical advice and emotional support. The Holy Spirit provided her with patience and endurance. Jessica now leads a support group for parents of special needs children, sharing her experiences and encouraging them to rely on God's strength.

These stories show how the Holy Spirit can change people and help them get through hard times. These people got the strength and direction they needed to get through their problems by praying, reading the Bible, asking for help from others, and believing in God's plan. Their stories give us hope and motivation because they show us that with the help of the Holy Spirit, we can get through anything and come out stronger in our faith.

Growth from Facing Challenges with Faith: Reframing Difficulties as Opportunities for Spiritual Development

In life, you will always have to deal with problems, but if you approach them with faith, they can become strong opportunities to grow spiritually. By seeing hardships as opportunities to grow, we can strengthen our relationship with God and our ability to handle them. This point of view can help you grow and become more spiritually mature in these ways.

Embracing Challenges as Part of God's Plan

Understanding that challenges are part of God's divine plan helps us view them as opportunities for growth. Romans

8:28 reminds us that "In all things, God works for the good of those who love him, who have been called according to his purpose." This verse encourages us to trust that even our difficulties have a purpose. Instead of seeing challenges as setbacks, we can embrace them as moments that God uses to shape and refine us.

Building Stronger Faith Through Trials

Trials test and strengthen our faith, much like a muscle that grows stronger with exercise. James 1:2-4 advises, "Consider it pure joy, my brothers and sisters, whenever you face trials of many kinds because you know that the testing of your faith produces perseverance. Let perseverance finish its work so that you may be mature and complete, not lacking anything." Each challenge we face with faith can increase our perseverance, making us more spiritually mature and resilient.

Developing a Deeper Dependence on God

Challenges often bring us to a point where we realize our limitations and our need for God. In 2 Corinthians 12:9, Paul shares God's response to his plea for relief from his challenges: "My grace is sufficient for you, for my power is made perfect in weakness." This profound truth teaches us that it is in our weaknesses and challenges that God's strength is most evident. When we depend more on Him, our relationship with Him deepens and becomes more intimate.

Cultivating Patience and Endurance

Facing difficulties with faith requires patience and endurance, qualities that are essential for spiritual growth. Romans 5:3-4 explains, "Not only so, but we also glory in our sufferings, because we know that suffering produces perseverance; perseverance, character; and character, hope." Patience and endurance built through trials fortify our character, making us more like Christ. These qualities help us to maintain hope and trust in God's timing and wisdom.

Enhancing Empathy and Compassion

Experiencing challenges firsthand makes us more empathetic and compassionate towards others. 2 Corinthians 1:3-4 says, "Praise be to the God and Father of our Lord Jesus Christ, the Father of compassion and the God of all comfort, who comforts us in all our troubles so that we can comfort those in any trouble with the comfort we ourselves receive from God." Our trials equip us to support and comfort others facing similar situations, enhancing our capacity for empathy and making our ministry to others more effective and heartfelt.

Reframing Difficulties as Learning Opportunities

Instead of viewing challenges as obstacles, we can reframe them as learning opportunities. Each difficulty can teach us valuable lessons about life, ourselves, and our faith. Proverbs 3:11-12 advises, "My son, do not despise the Lord's discipline and do not resent his rebuke, because the

Lord disciplines those he loves, as a father the son he delights in." God uses these experiences to correct, instruct, and guide us toward a deeper understanding of His will and purpose for our lives.

Strengthening Your Prayer Life

Challenges often drive us to our knees, enhancing our prayer life. When we face situations beyond our control, we pray to God, seeking His guidance and intervention. Philippians 4:6-7 encourages, "Do not be anxious about anything, but in every situation, by prayer and petition, with thanksgiving, present your requests to God. And the peace of God, which transcends all understanding, will guard your hearts and your minds in Christ Jesus." Through prayer, we can experience God's peace and presence, strengthening our spiritual connection.

Encouraging Humility and Surrender

Difficulties remind us of our dependence on God, fostering humility and surrender. In 1 Peter 5:6-7, we are instructed, "Humble yourselves, therefore, under God's mighty hand, that he may lift you up in due time. Cast all your anxiety on him because he cares for you." Acknowledging our need for God's help cultivates a humble heart and willingness to surrender our lives to His will, which is critical to spiritual maturity.

Building a Testimony of Faith

Each challenge we overcome with faith builds our testimony, providing a powerful witness to God's faithfulness. Revelation 12:11 says, "They triumphed over him by the blood of the Lamb and by the word of their testimony." Sharing our stories of overcoming adversity can inspire and encourage others, demonstrating the power of faith and the Holy Spirit in our lives. Our testimonies serve as a reminder of God's unwavering presence and His ability to bring good out of even the most challenging circumstances.

Finding Joy on the Journey

Finally, learning to find joy amidst challenges is a profound aspect of spiritual growth. Habakkuk 3:17-18 beautifully expresses this sentiment: "Though the fig tree does not bud and there are no grapes on the vines, though the olive crop fails and the fields produce no food, though there are no sheep in the pen and no cattle in the stalls, yet I will rejoice in the Lord, I will be joyful in God my Savior." This joy is not dependent on circumstances but is rooted in our relationship with God and our hope in Him.

The Importance of Daily Renewal and Staying Vigilant Against Deception

In our journey of faith, daily renewal and vigilance against deception are crucial. These practices help maintain a strong spiritual foundation and protect us from the subtle influences that can lead us astray. Here's why daily renewal is essential and how to stay vigilant against deception.

The Necessity of Daily Renewal

Daily renewal is continually refreshing our spiritual lives, ensuring our faith remains vibrant and active. Romans 12:2 emphasizes the importance of this practice: "Do not conform to the pattern of this world but be transformed by the renewing of your mind. Then you will be able to test and approve what God's will is—his good, pleasing, and perfect will." This transformation requires consistent effort, as the pressures and influences of the world are relentless.

Daily renewal involves several key practices. Firstly, spending time in prayer allows us to communicate with God, express our gratitude, seek guidance, and find comfort in His presence. Prayer helps align our hearts with God's will, providing the strength and wisdom needed to navigate daily challenges.

Secondly, engaging with Scripture is vital. The Bible is God's living word, offering guidance, correction, and encouragement. By reading and meditating on Scripture daily, we fill our minds with God's truths, which fortify us against the lies and deceptions of the world. Psalm 119:105 reminds us, "Your word is a lamp for my feet, a light on my path." This daily immersion in God's word illuminates our way and strengthens our resolve to live according to His principles.

Thirdly, worship and gratitude are integral to daily renewal. Expressing thanks to God for His blessings and worshiping Him for His goodness shifts our focus from our problems to His greatness. This practice cultivates a heart of gratitude and joy, which is essential for a resilient faith.

Staying Vigilant Against Deception

While daily renewal strengthens our spiritual foundation, staying vigilant against deception ensures we remain on the right path. Deception can come in many forms, from subtle lies that distort the truth to blatant falsehoods that lead us away from God.

1 Peter 5:8 warns us, "Be alert and of sober mind. Your enemy, the devil, prowls around like a roaring lion looking for someone to devour." This verse underscores the need for constant vigilance. Here are some strategies to guard against deception:

1. Know the Truth:

To discern deception, we must first know the truth. This involves a deep and thorough understanding of Scripture. Jesus said in John 8:31-32, "If you hold to my teaching, you are really my disciples. Then you will know the truth, and the truth will set you free." Knowing the truth of God's word equips us to recognize and reject falsehoods.

2. Pray for Discernment:

Discernment is a gift of the Holy Spirit that helps us distinguish between truth and error. James 1:5 encourages us to ask God for wisdom: "If any of you lacks wisdom, you should ask God, who gives generously to all without finding fault, and it will be given to you." Regularly praying for discernment sharpens our ability to detect deception.

3. Test the Spirits:

1 John 4:1 advises, "Dear friends, do not believe every spirit, but test the spirits to see whether they are from God, because many false prophets have gone out into the world." This means evaluating teachings and messages against the truth of Scripture. If something contradicts God's word, it is not from Him.

4. Stay Connected to the Faith Community:

Isolation can make us more vulnerable to deception. Staying connected to a community of believers provides accountability and support. Hebrews 10:24-25 emphasizes the importance of fellowship: "And let us consider how we may spur one another on toward love and good deeds, not giving up meeting together, as some are in the habit of doing, but encouraging one another—and all the more as you see the Day approaching." Regular interaction with other believers helps us stay grounded in our faith.

5. Be Aware of Subtle Influences:

Deception often starts subtly. We must be aware of the media we consume, the company we keep, and the ideologies we entertain. Philippians 4:8 advises, "Finally, brothers and sisters, whatever is true, whatever is noble, whatever is right, whatever is pure, whatever is lovely, whatever is admirable—if anything is excellent or praiseworthy—think about such things." Focusing on what is good and true helps guard our hearts and minds against deceit.

6. Cultivate Humility:

Pride can close our eyes to deception. Cultivating humility helps us remain teachable and open to correction. Proverbs 11:2 states, "When pride comes, then comes disgrace, but with humility comes wisdom." A humble heart is more likely to seek and accept the truth.

7. Regular Self-Examination:

Regularly examining our beliefs and actions in light of Scripture helps us stay on course. 2 Corinthians 13:5 urges, "Examine yourselves to see whether you are in the faith; test yourselves. Do you not realize that Christ Jesus is in you—unless, of course, you fail the test?" Self-examination ensures we remain aligned with God's truth.

To keep your faith strong and resilient, you need to renew it every day and be on the lookout for lies. We can grow spiritually and avoid being tricked by committing to daily prayer, reading the Bible, worshipping, seeking insight, staying connected to the faith community, being aware of subtle influences, practicing humility, and regularly examining ourselves. These habits keep us close to God, help us deal with life's problems wisely, and help us live in line with what His word says.

-*When you know God by his spirit*

Only the spirit of God knows man's thoughts

So, you are never alone when you become saved or born again. You have the Spirit of God or the Holy Spirit living on the inside of you, so you are just a breath away from God being with you. Through a relationship with the Holy Spirit, we can have Intimacy with our creator on a spiritual level.

-*Our relationship goes far beyond salvation.*

When we spend time with God, His character starts to rub off on us. That's why God wants to spend time with you so you will become more like him (Draw near to God, and He will draw near to you.) God wants to spend time with you. We become godlier through an intimate through an intimate knowledge of God.

Chapter 7: Sharing Your Faith with Others

Sharing your faith is a vital aspect of living a life guided by the Holy Spirit. It's not just a responsibility; it's a privilege that brings deep rewards to both you and those with whom you share. This chapter delves into the importance of sharing your faith, focusing on the positive impact it can have on your life and the lives of others.

The Positive Impact on You

1. Strengthening Your Faith: When you share your faith, you reinforce your own beliefs and understanding of the gospel. Talking to others compels you to delve deeper into your own knowledge of scripture and personal experiences with God. This process not only strengthens your faith but also brings clarity and deeper conviction.

2. Building Confidence: Sharing your faith can initially be intimidating, but with each encounter, your confidence grows. The Holy Spirit empowers you, giving you the words to speak and the courage to speak them. Over time, you will find that sharing your faith becomes a natural and joyful part of your life.

3. Experiencing Joy: Knowing that you have contributed to someone's spiritual journey is incredibly fulfilling. It reminds you of the gospel's transformative power and the eternal significance of your efforts.

4. Deepening Your Relationship with God: As you share your faith, you rely more on the Holy Spirit for guidance, wisdom, and boldness. This dependence deepens your relationship with God as you experience His faithfulness and provision in new ways. You will find yourself growing in trust and intimacy with the Holy Spirit.

The Positive Impact on Others

1. Offering Hope: Many people are searching for meaning and hope in their lives. By sharing your faith, you offer them the hope found in Jesus Christ. You allow them to experience the peace, joy, and purpose that comes from a relationship with God.

2. Encouraging Transformation: Your testimony can be a powerful catalyst for change in someone's life. Hearing how God has worked in your life can inspire others to seek the same transformation. Your story can be the bridge that leads them to explore faith and ultimately find their path to God.

3. Building Community: As more people come to faith, they become part of the body of Christ, contributing to a vibrant and supportive community. This community provides mutual encouragement, accountability, and spiritual growth.

4. Spreading Love: At its core, sharing your faith is an act of love. It is about caring enough for others to share with them the most important and life-changing truth you know. This love reflects the heart of God and can have a ripple effect, spreading kindness, compassion, and hope throughout your community.

Overcoming Challenges in Sharing Your Faith

While sharing your faith is incredibly rewarding, it can also come with challenges. Fear of rejection, feelings of inadequacy, or not knowing what to say are common obstacles. However, with the Holy Spirit's guidance and a few practical strategies, you can overcome these challenges.

1. Pray for Boldness: Ask the Holy Spirit to give you the courage to share your faith. Pray for opportunities and the right words to say. Trust that God will equip you for the task He has called you to.

2. Start with Your Story: Your testimony is a powerful tool. Share how Jesus has changed your life. Be honest and authentic; people are often more receptive to genuine experiences than theological arguments.

3. Listen and Respond: Sharing your faith is not just about talking; it's also about listening. Pay attention to the needs and concerns of the person you are speaking with. Show empathy and address their questions and doubts with kindness and understanding.

4. Use Scripture: The Bible is a powerful resource. Share relevant scriptures that speak to the issues or questions being discussed. God's word has the power to convict and transform hearts.

5. Live Out Your Faith: Your actions often speak louder than words. Live in a way that reflects the love and character of Christ. Your integrity, kindness, and compassion can open doors for conversations about your faith.

Practical Ways to Share Your Faith

1. Build Relationships: Invest in relationships with people who do not yet know Christ. Show genuine interest in their lives and build trust. Faithful conversations often happen naturally within the context of a strong relationship.

2. Be Ready to Share: 1 Peter 3:15 encourages us to be prepared to answer everyone who asks why we have hope. Be ready to share your faith at any time, whether through a casual conversation, a social media post, or an act of kindness.

3. Use Your Gifts: God has given you unique gifts and talents. Use them to share your faith. Whether it's through music, art, writing, or serving others, find creative ways to express and share the gospel.

4. Involve Your Church: Partner with your church community in evangelism efforts. Participate in outreach events, mission trips, or community service projects. Working together with other believers can provide support and encouragement.

5. Respect Differences: Share your faith with respect and sensitivity. Recognize that everyone is on their journey and may have different beliefs and backgrounds. Approach conversations with love, not judgment, and be open to listening, learning, and sharing.

Practical tips for talking with Jesus practically

Talking about Jesus can evoke deep satisfaction but can also be intimidating. A lot of people worry that they will seem harsh or pushy. Here are some useful tips that will help you talk about your faith naturally and surely:

Focus on building real relationships before talking about your faith. Be a good friend by being interested in other people's lives and stories. When people feel like you care about them, they are more open to talking about faith.

Be honest about your faith. Talk about your relationship with Jesus and how it changed your life. Being open and honest can help people connect with you more deeply and understand what you're saying.

Listening is just as important as saying when it comes to communicating well. Listen to what other people are saying and answer with care. You can have a useful conversation with someone if you listen to what they have to say.

Please don't use too much religious jargon that people who don't believe in it might find hard to understand or offensive. Instead, talk about your religion in everyday language. This makes it easy for people to understand your message.

Stories make people feel something. Tell stories from your own life that show how Jesus has changed things.

Personal stories are strong ways to get your point across in a way that people will find interesting and relatable.

To get people involved, ask open-ended questions about their thoughts and experiences. You can start a deeper talk without being too pushy by asking, "What do you think about faith?" or "Have you ever had a spiritual experience?"

Know that each person has their path. Don't judge them, and listen to what they have to say. Listen to what they have to say and try to find shared ground. This method helps people accept and understand each other.

It often takes a while to talk about faith. Wait your turn and let the conversation flow freely. Do not share everything right away. Allow the Holy Spirit to lead the talk, and be ready for where it takes you.

When you talk to people, stress Jesus's love and kindness. Talk about how His lessons have improved your life. People want to hear signs of love, acceptance, and hope.

A lot of the time, actions speak louder than words. Use your deeds to show how much you believe. Always be kind, caring, and honest in your daily life. People are more likely to be interested and willing to talk about your faith if they see how it helps them.

Be ready to talk about your faith if someone asks. Read the Bible and make sure you know your views well enough to explain them. You can say you don't know the answer and offer to find out.

When it makes sense, use the Bible to support your points. Pick texts that will help you and are simple to understand. Discuss how certain parts of the Bible have helped you.

Before and during your talks, pray for wisdom and direction. Ask the Holy Spirit to help you find the right words and way to say them. You can trust that God will use you to reach other people.

If it works with the discussion, offer to pray with them. It can be very strong to show your faith and care about their worries and well-being in this way.

In the end, you should accept the other person's choice, whether they agree with your faith or not. Do not stop being loving and kind, no matter what happens. Remember that sharing is your job; God changes people's hearts.

You don't have to be scared or angry when you talk about Jesus. You can share your faith easily and confidently if you build real relationships, are honest, listen, and value different points of view. Focus on love and kindness, show your faith in what you do, and let the Holy Spirit lead the way you talk to people. You can make a difference without coming across as pushy or critical if you follow these useful tips.

There are several important steps you need to take to use your own experience to inspire others and make your life story into a strong testimony. By being honest and open about your journey, you can connect deeply with others and give them hope and support. Here are some good ways to write and give your testimony:

Start by **reflecting on your life** and **identifying pivotal moments** significantly impacting your faith journey. These moments could include challenges, breakthroughs, or specific instances where you experienced God's presence and guidance. Write down these experiences, focusing on the emotions, struggles, and eventual outcomes. Being honest and transparent about your journey, including the highs and lows, is crucial.

"Come and hear, all you who fear God; let me tell you what he has done for me." (Psalm 66:16)

When crafting your testimony, structure it to **highlight transformation**. Begin with your life before you encountered Jesus or experienced a significant spiritual awakening. Describe the struggles, doubts, or emptiness you felt. This helps others understand the context and relatability of your story. For example, you might share how you struggled with anxiety or lacked purpose before finding faith.

"Therefore, if anyone is in Christ, the new creation has come: The old has gone, the new is here!" (2 Corinthians 5:17)

Next, **transition to the turning point** in your story. Describe the moment or process that led to your encounter with Jesus or a significant spiritual experience. This could be a dramatic event, a gradual realization, or a series of smaller moments that culminated in a profound change. Explain how you felt during this time and what specifically drew you towards faith. For instance, you might recount a moment of prayer, a conversation with a mentor, or an inspiring scripture passage that resonated with you.

"I sought the Lord, and he answered me; he delivered me from all my fears." (Psalm 34:4)

After detailing your turning point, **focus on the transformation** that followed. Explain how your life changed after you embraced faith. Share specific examples of how your relationship with God has impacted your daily life, relationships, and overall outlook. Highlight the positive changes, such as increased peace, purpose, joy, or a sense of belonging. Use concrete examples to illustrate these changes, such as overcoming a specific fear, finding direction in your career, or experiencing restored relationships.

"For we are God's handiwork, created in Christ Jesus to do good works, which God prepared in advance for us to do." (Ephesians 2:10)

To make your testimony even more powerful, **include ongoing experiences** of how your faith continues to shape your life. Share recent stories of God's faithfulness, answered prayers, or moments of spiritual growth. This demonstrates that your faith is an ongoing journey, not just a past event. It also encourages others to see their spiritual journey as dynamic and evolving.

"And we know that in all things God works for the good of those who love him, who have been called according to his purpose." (Romans 8:28)

When sharing your testimony, it's important to be **relatable and empathetic**. Acknowledge that everyone's journey is unique and that your story is just one example of how faith can transform a life. Avoid coming across as preachy or judgmental. Instead, focus on sharing your experiences and how they have shaped you. Be open to listening to others' stories and finding common ground.

Incorporate scripture and spiritual insights to provide a solid foundation for your testimony. Relate your experiences to biblical principles and truths that have guided you. This not only reinforces the authenticity of your story but also connects it to a larger narrative of faith that others can relate to.

"Your word is a lamp for my feet, a light on my path."

(Psalm 119:105)

As you share your testimony, **consider the context** and audience. Adapt your story to fit the setting: a one-on-one conversation, a small group meeting, or a larger public forum. Be mindful of the time and attention span of your audience. While it's important to share significant details, keep your testimony concise and focused.

Practice sharing your testimony to gain confidence and clarity. You can rehearse with a trusted friend or mentor who can provide feedback. Pay attention to your tone, body language, and overall delivery. Being prepared helps you communicate your story effectively and authentically.

Using your personal experience to inspire others through your testimony is a powerful way to share the love and transformative power of Jesus. By being authentic, relatable, and empathetic, you can offer hope and encouragement to those seeking faith and purpose in their own lives.

Being a positive influence in your community is essential to living out your faith. As followers of Jesus, we are called to be the salt and light of the world (Matthew 5:13-16), bringing hope, love, and positive change to those around us. Our faith not only transforms us internally but also compels us to act in ways that positively impact our communities. Here's why and how faith can lead to meaningful actions that benefit everyone.

Faith provides a moral and ethical framework that guides our actions and interactions with others. The teachings of Jesus emphasize love, compassion, and service. By following these principles, we can become a source of positivity and support within our communities. For example, Jesus' command to "love your neighbor as yourself" (Mark 12:31) encourages us to care for those around us, regardless of their background or circumstances. This foundational principle drives us to act with kindness and generosity, fostering a sense of unity and support within our communities.

One of the most significant ways faith can lead to meaningful actions is through acts of service. Serving others is a tangible expression of our faith and a way to demonstrate God's love in action. Whether it's volunteering at a local shelter, participating in community clean-ups, or providing meals for those in need, acts of service can have a profound impact. These actions not only meet immediate needs but also build bridges and foster a sense of belonging and community. Jesus himself modeled this servant leadership, stating, "The Son of Man did not come to be served, but to serve" (Matthew 20:28).

It also inspires us to pursue justice and advocate for those who are marginalized or oppressed. Throughout the Bible, we see a consistent call to defend the rights of the poor and vulnerable. Proverbs 31:8-9 urges us to "speak up for those who cannot speak for themselves, for the rights of all who are destitute." This call to action compels us to address social injustices and work towards a fairer and more equitable society. Whether it's through supporting policies that promote social justice, participating in peaceful protests, or raising awareness about important issues, our faith motivates us to be a voice for the voiceless and to seek justice for all.

Another significant aspect of being a positive influence is through building and nurturing relationships within our communities. Faith encourages us to form meaningful connections with others, breaking down barriers of prejudice and fostering genuine understanding and respect. By engaging in open and respectful dialogue, we can learn from each other's experiences and work together towards common goals. The apostle Paul reminds us to "be devoted to one another in love. Honor one another above yourselves" (Romans 12:10). This relational approach helps to create a strong, supportive network within the community, where everyone feels valued and included.

Faith also equips us with the strength and resilience needed to face challenges and adversity. Life is filled with difficulties, but our faith provides us with hope and the assurance that we are not alone. This resilience is not just for personal benefit but is a source of inspiration for others. By remaining steadfast and hopeful in the face of trials, we can offer encouragement and support to those who are struggling. Our ability to endure and thrive despite hardships can serve as a powerful testimony to the strength and hope that faith provides.

Faith-based initiatives and organizations play a crucial role in community development and support. Churches, faith-based charities, and other religious organizations often spearhead programs that address various community needs, such as food banks, educational programs, and healthcare services. These initiatives not only provide essential resources but also create opportunities for individuals to come together and contribute to the common good. By participating in or supporting these organizations, we can amplify our positive impact and reach more needy people.

In addition to practical actions, our attitudes and behaviors can significantly influence our communities. By embodying the fruits of the Spirit—love, joy, peace, patience, kindness, goodness, faithfulness, gentleness, and self-control (Galatians 5:22-23)—we can create an environment that reflects the values of the Kingdom of God. Our interactions, whether in person or online, can be characterized by grace and truth, setting a positive example for others to follow.

Sharing faith can be a daunting task for many believers, often accompanied by fears and obstacles that can seem impossible. However, addressing these concerns with encouragement and practical solutions can empower you to share your faith more confidently and effectively. Here, we'll explore some common fears and obstacles in sharing faith and offer ways to overcome them.

One of the most common fears is the fear of rejection. Many people worry that sharing their faith will lead to social alienation or damaged relationships. It's important to remember that Jesus himself faced rejection and instructed his followers to expect the same. In John 15:18, Jesus says, "If the world hates you, keep in mind that it hated me first." Understanding that rejection is not a reflection of personal failure, but a possible response to the message can help alleviate this fear. Practically, approach conversations with respect and sensitivity, focusing on building genuine relationships. This can create an environment where people feel valued and respected, even if they don't immediately accept your message.

Another significant obstacle is the fear of not knowing enough. Many believers feel they lack the theological knowledge or eloquence to share their faith effectively.

However, the story of the blind man healed by Jesus in John 9:25 is a powerful reminder that personal experience can be just as impactful as deep theological knowledge. The man simply stated, "One thing I do know. I was blind but now I see!" Sharing your personal story of how Jesus has transformed your life can be incredibly compelling. Additionally, continually seek to grow in your understanding of scripture and theology. Engaging in Bible studies, reading Christian literature, and participating in church teachings can equip you with the knowledge and confidence to share your faith more effectively.

Fear of being perceived as pushy or judgmental is another common concern. To overcome this, focus on sharing your faith through acts of love and service. In Matthew 5:16, Jesus says, "Let your light shine before others, that they may see your good deeds and glorify your Father in heaven."

By living out your faith in tangible ways, you can demonstrate the love of Christ without coming across as aggressive. When conversations about faith arise, be gentle and respectful, listening as much as you speak. This approach fosters open dialogue and shows that you genuinely care about the other person's perspective.

A practical obstacle is finding the right opportunity to share your faith. Many people struggle with when and how to bring up spiritual topics in conversation. Pray for divine appointments and be attentive to the Holy Spirit's prompting. Colossians 4:5- 6 advises, "Be wise in the way you act toward outsiders; make the most of every opportunity. Let your conversation be always full of grace, seasoned with salt, so that you may know how to answer everyone."

Look for natural openings in conversations, such as when someone shares a personal struggle or asks about your weekend activities. Share how your faith plays a role in your life, and be ready to offer words of hope and encouragement.

Another obstacle is the fear of difficult questions. It's normal to feel anxious about not having all the answers. Remember that it's okay to admit when you don't know something. In 1 Peter 3:15, we are encouraged to "Always be prepared to give an answer to everyone who asks you to give the reason for the hope that you have. But do this with gentleness and respect."

If you encounter a question you can't answer, acknowledge it honestly and offer to find out more. This shows humility and a willingness to learn, which can enhance your credibility and foster deeper conversations.

Feelings of inadequacy can also hinder you from sharing your faith. You might believe you're not spiritually mature enough or your life isn't a perfect example of Christian living. It's important to remember that God uses imperfect people to accomplish His purposes. In 2 Corinthians 12:9, God tells Paul, "My grace is sufficient for you, for my power is made perfect in weakness."

Trust that God can work through your weaknesses and that your authenticity and transparency can make your testimony even more relatable and impactful.

It's essential to address the spiritual warfare aspect of sharing faith. Ephesians 6:12 reminds us that "Our struggle is not against flesh and blood but against the rulers, against the authorities, against the powers of this dark world and against the spiritual forces of evil in the heavenly realms." Prayer is a powerful tool in overcoming this obstacle.

Pray for courage, wisdom, and opportunities to share your faith. Surround yourself with a supportive community of believers who can encourage and pray for you.

Expressing your beliefs creatively and respectfully can positively influence those around you and demonstrate the impact of your faith. Here are examples of how to share your beliefs in various settings, from school to work to social media.

At School

1. Leading by Example: One of the most effective ways to express your beliefs in school is through your actions. Demonstrate kindness, integrity, and respect in your interactions with classmates and teachers. When others see the positive difference in your behavior, they may be curious about the source of your values.

2. Starting or Joining Faith-Based Clubs: Many schools allow students to form or join faith-based clubs.

These groups provide a supportive environment for discussing faith, organizing events, and serving the community. For example, you might organize a charity drive or volunteer event that aligns with your beliefs, showcasing the principles of service and compassion.

3. Sharing Personal Stories in Class Assignments: When appropriate, incorporate your beliefs into class assignments, such as essays, presentations, or projects. For instance, you might write a paper on how your faith influences your view on social issues or share a personal testimony during a speech. This allows you to express your beliefs thoughtfully and contextually.

At Work

4. Ethical Conduct: Demonstrate your beliefs through your work ethic and conduct. Be honest, reliable, and fair in your dealings. Your consistent integrity and professionalism can inspire curiosity about your values.

5. Volunteering and Charity: Suggest team-building activities that involve volunteering or charity work. For example, organize a group to serve at a local food bank or participate in a charity run. These activities allow you to live out your faith while fostering team spirit.

6. Respectful Conversations: Be open to discussing your beliefs during appropriate times, such as lunch breaks or casual conversations. Share personal stories about how your faith guides your decisions and actions, always listening respectfully to others' perspectives.

7. Celebrating Holidays: Share about religious holidays and their significance in a non-intrusive way. For example, bring treats to celebrate a religious holiday and explain its importance to those who are interested. This can open up conversations about your faith naturally and inclusively.

On social media

8. Inspirational Quotes and Verses: Share Bible verses, inspirational quotes, or personal reflections on your social media profiles. For instance, post a verse that has been meaningful to you, accompanied by a brief explanation of its impact on your life.

9. Blogging or Vlogging: Start a blog or YouTube channel where you discuss your faith journey, share insights from scripture, or talk about how your beliefs shape your daily life. Ensure your content is respectful, engaging, and open to dialogue.

10. Supporting Positive Causes: Use your platform to support causes that align with your beliefs, such as promoting social justice, charity work, or community service. Share stories and updates about your involvement, highlighting the connection to your faith.

11. Engaging Respectfully: Engage in respectful conversations about faith on social media. Respond kindly to comments, even if they are critical. Show grace and patience, aiming to understand different viewpoints while clearly articulating your own.

General Practices Across Settings

12. Acts of Kindness: Perform random acts of kindness and let your actions speak for your faith. Whether you help a neighbor, support a colleague, or volunteer in your community, these acts can demonstrate the love and compassion central to your beliefs.

13. Listening and Learning: Approach conversations about faith with a listening ear. Show genuine interest in others' beliefs and experiences. This mutual respect can open doors for deeper discussions about your faith.

14. Sharing Resources: Offer books, podcasts, or articles that have inspired you. For instance, if a colleague is facing a tough time, you might share a book that has provided you comfort. Be mindful of sharing resources that are relevant and sensitive to the other person's situation.

15. Creating Safe Spaces: Foster environments where open discussions about faith are welcomed and respected. Whether it's in a school club, a workplace group, or an online forum, create a space where people can share their beliefs without fear of judgment.

16. Prayer and Meditation: In times of crisis or need, offer to pray for or with others if they are comfortable. This can be a powerful way to share your faith and show support. Respect their response, and even if they decline, continue to offer your support in other ways.

17. Personal Invitations: Invite friends, colleagues, or classmates to faith-based events, such as church services, youth groups, or community service projects. Make sure the invitation is open and without pressure, and respect their decision whether to accept or decline.

18. Celebrating Diversity: Celebrate the diversity of beliefs and cultures around you. Acknowledge and respect different religious holidays and customs, showing that you value and appreciate the faith journeys of others.

Loving all people, including Jews, is a fundamental aspect of the Christian faith that reflects the heart of Jesus' teachings and the essence of God's love. As Christians, we are called to embody this love in our daily lives, demonstrating compassion, respect, and kindness to everyone, regardless of their background or beliefs. This inclusive love is not just an option but a core mandate of our faith, deeply rooted in the teachings of the Bible.

Jesus Himself modeled this inclusive love throughout His ministry. In the Gospels, we see Him interacting with people from all walks of life, including Jews, Samaritans, Romans, and many others. He broke down cultural and religious barriers, showing that God's love is universal and not confined to a specific group. One of the most poignant examples is Jesus' interaction with the Samaritan woman at the well (John 4:1-26). Despite the deep-seated hatred between Jews and Samaritans, Jesus engaged her in a meaningful conversation, offering her the living water of eternal life.

The Apostle Paul also emphasized the importance of loving and accepting all people. In his letter to the Galatians, he writes, "There is neither Jew nor Gentile, neither slave nor free, nor is there male and female, for you are all one in Christ Jesus" (Galatians 3:28). This verse underscores the idea that in Christ, all human distinctions fade away, and we are united as one family. This unity is a powerful testament to the transformative power of God's love and the inclusive nature of the Christian faith.

Moreover, Christians have a special historical and spiritual connection with the Jewish people. The roots of Christianity are deeply intertwined with Judaism. Jesus Himself was Jewish, and the early Christian church emerged from the Jewish community. The Old Testament, a significant part of the Christian Bible, is the Hebrew Scriptures, revered and respected by Jews and Christians. This shared heritage calls us to honor and love the Jewish people as part of our spiritual family.

Loving all people, including Jews, also aligns with the Great Commandment that Jesus highlighted: "Love the Lord your God with all your heart and with all your soul and with all your mind" and "Love your neighbor as yourself" (Matthew 22:37-39). This commandment encapsulates the essence of Christian ethics and calls us to extend our love to everyone, reflecting God's unconditional love for humanity.

In practical terms, loving all people means actively overcoming prejudice, discrimination, and hatred. It means standing against anti-Semitism and any form of bigotry, advocating for justice, and promoting peace and understanding. It involves educating ourselves about the history, culture, and beliefs of others, including the Jewish community, to build bridges of respect and mutual appreciation.

Let us remember that our faith calls us to be ambassadors of God's love by loving all people, including the Jews. We live out the true essence of Christianity. This love is not passive but active, challenging us to reach out, build relationships, and promote unity in our diverse world. Through this love, we fulfill Jesus' command to be the light of the world, shining brightly in a world that desperately needs the hope and healing that only God's love can bring.

In loving all people, we reflect the heart of our faith and the character of our Savior. Let us commit to this high calling, striving to love unconditionally and inclusively, just as God loves us.

Don't Grieve the Holy Spirit

When you become so sensitive to the Holy Spirit, it's hard to be around people who use bad language. Even television is bad now with the horrible language.

We must not forget the Holy Spirit lives inside of us. Don't bring him into a situation where you know the holy spirit will grieve; he will become quiet.

If you cause the spirit to grieve or sorrow, you must immediately ask for forgiveness and make it a sincere apology.

Chapter 8: Your Future with the Holy Spirit

Every one of us is part of something greater than we can fully understand. This belief is rooted in the idea that God has a unique plan for each person's life. It's a plan that holds mystery and excitement, guiding us through our journey with purpose and intention. This divine design is not something we can predict or control but something we are invited to trust and embrace. As Jeremiah 29:11 reminds us, *"For I know the plans I have for you," declares the Lord, "plans to prosper you and not to harm you, plans to give you hope and a future."*

The idea of a personal plan crafted by God brings comfort. It reassures us that we are not facing life on our own. Even in times of confusion or uncertainty, there is a direction and a purpose that is unfolding. We may not always see the full path ahead, but we can be assured that a plan exists. This understanding gives us hope, knowing each step is part of a bigger picture.

What makes God's plan so intriguing is its mysterious nature. We are often drawn to solving puzzles and understanding how things fit together. God's plan for our lives is much like a puzzle, where we can only see a piece at a time. We may wonder why certain events happen or why we are led down particular paths, but in time, the pieces come together. The mystery lies in not knowing how our journey will unfold, but the excitement is in trusting that it will lead to a place of fulfillment and joy.

A compelling example of God's mysterious and redemptive plan can be seen in the story of the demoniacs. Two men lived in a graveyard, possessed by demons so fierce and uncontrollable that no one could restrain them. One of these men was tormented by so many demons that they called themselves 'Legion,' signifying their overwhelming number. This man, under the influence of these demons, roamed around naked, crying out and harming himself with stones, completely cut off from society. When Jesus encountered them, the demons recognized His authority and begged Him to send them into a nearby herd of pigs rather than cast them into the abyss. Jesus granted their request, and as the demons entered the pigs, the entire herd rushed down a steep bank into a lake and drowned.

This powerful act of deliverance not only freed the men from their torment but demonstrated Jesus' supreme authority over the spiritual realm. It shows that God's plan always works for our good, even when situations seem hopeless. Just as Jesus intervened in the lives of these men, bringing them from chaos to peace, God has the power to transform our lives, guiding us toward His purpose. The transformation of the demoniacs shows that no matter how bound or broken we may feel, God's plan includes redemption and freedom, inviting us to trust in His power and love.

The Holy Spirit's role is crucial in revealing this plan. The Holy Spirit is our guide, providing the wisdom and insight to address life's twists and turns. Through whispers, gentle nudges, and moments of clarity, the Holy Spirit helps us discern the steps we should take. While we may not see the entire plan, the Holy Spirit lights the path just enough to keep us moving forward with confidence.

Living in alignment with God's plan requires us to let go of our need to control every aspect of our lives. It challenges us to trust God's timing and wisdom, even when we don't understand what is happening. This trust is not passive; it's an active engagement with the Holy Spirit. It involves listening, seeking, and being open to where we are led. Each decision, each experience, and each relationship is a part of the unfolding plan.

The excitement of this journey comes from the unexpected turns it can take. God's plan is not always predictable, but it is always purposeful. We may find ourselves in unexpected situations, meeting people who change our perspectives, or facing challenges that strengthen our faith. These moments, joyful or difficult, are all part of how God shapes us and prepares us for what is to come. The excitement lies in discovering new aspects of ourselves and our faith, realizing that we are capable of more than we ever imagined.

The most reassuring aspect of God's plan is that it is tailored to each individual. No two plans are the same, just as no two people are the same. God knows us intimately— our strengths, weaknesses, dreams, and fears. He creates a plan that fits us perfectly and aligns with who we are and who we are meant to become. This uniqueness ensures that our journey is meaningful and personal, tailored to lead us to our true purpose.

When we consider our future with the Holy Spirit, we are invited to embrace both the mystery and excitement of God's plan. We can rest in the knowledge that our lives have a purpose, and each day brings us closer to fulfilling that purpose. By trusting in the Holy Spirit's guidance and being open to the unfolding journey, we can walk confidently and joyfully, knowing that God's plan for us is filled with love, hope, and promise.

To fully experience this journey and remain aligned with God's purpose, it's essential to maintain a strong connection with the Holy Spirit. This connection is not automatic; it requires deliberate effort and cultivating spiritual habits.

Practical Ways to Stay Connected to the Holy Spirit Long-Term

Staying connected to the Holy Spirit is essential for living a life that aligns with God's purpose. It requires more than occasional prayer or sporadic moments of reflection. Building lasting spiritual habits is the key to maintaining a continuous relationship with the Holy Spirit. These habits anchor us, helping us stay connected even when life gets busy or challenging. Here are practical ways to ensure a long-term, consistent connection with the Holy Spirit.

1. Daily Prayer: Prayer is one of the most effective ways to communicate with the Holy Spirit. Setting aside specific times each day for prayer helps establish a routine. Begin your day by inviting the Holy Spirit into your heart and asking for guidance. Simple prayers of gratitude, requests for help, or seeking wisdom can open your heart to the Holy Spirit's presence. By making prayer a daily habit, you create a space where the Holy Spirit can communicate with you, guide your thoughts, and influence your decisions.

2. Reading Scripture Regularly: The Bible is the primary way the Holy Spirit speaks to us. Regularly reading Scripture allows the Holy Spirit to reveal God's truth to us. Establish a habit of reading a portion of the Bible each day. The key is consistency, whether it's a chapter or a few verses. Ask the Holy Spirit to give you understanding and insight as you read. Reflect on what the passages mean for your life and how to apply them. Over time, these readings will strengthen your connection with the Holy Spirit, offering guidance and encouragement.

3. Meditation and Reflection: Taking time to meditate and reflect is crucial for staying connected to the Holy Spirit. Find a quiet place to sit and reflect on God's presence. Focus on a particular scripture or a thought, or simply be still and allow the Holy Spirit to speak to your heart. Meditation helps quiet the noise of daily life and allows the Holy Spirit to guide your inner thoughts. In these moments of stillness, you can feel the Holy Spirit's comforting presence and hear His gentle whispers.

4. Worship: Engaging in regular worship, individually and with others, is a powerful way to stay connected to the Holy Spirit. Worship is not limited to singing; it can be expressed through prayer, reading psalms, or even quiet reflection on God's greatness. Worship shifts our focus away from ourselves and onto God. It reminds us of His power, love, and the role of the Holy Spirit in our lives. Make worship a regular part of your routine, not just on Sundays but throughout the week, to maintain a vibrant connection with the Holy Spirit.

5. Fellowship with Other Believers: Connecting with other believers is essential for spiritual growth and maintaining a relationship with the Holy Spirit. Join a church group, Bible study, or community where you can share your faith journey. These interactions provide support, encouragement, and accountability. When you are surrounded by others who seek to follow the Holy Spirit, it strengthens your resolve and deepens your connection. Sharing experiences, praying for one another, and studying God's Word together fosters a deeper awareness of the Holy Spirit's work in your life.

6. Journaling: Writing down your thoughts, prayers, and experiences is a practical way to stay connected to the Holy Spirit. Keeping a spiritual journal allows you to track your journey, see patterns in how the Holy Spirit guides you, and reflect on your spiritual growth. Journaling helps you to articulate your thoughts and feelings, making it easier to identify where the Holy Spirit is leading you. By regularly writing, you become more attuned to the subtle ways the Holy Spirit influences your life.

7. Acts of Service: Engaging in acts of service is a powerful way to connect with the Holy Spirit. By serving others, you live out the love and compassion the Holy Spirit instills in your heart. Find ways to help those in need, whether it's volunteering at a local charity, helping a neighbor, or simply offering a listening ear to someone who is struggling. Through service, you allow the Holy Spirit to work through you, blessing others and reinforcing the values of kindness and love.

8. Confession and Forgiveness: Maintaining a relationship with the Holy Spirit requires a heart free from bitterness and resentment. Regularly practice confession to clear your heart of anything hindering your connection with God. Be honest about your mistakes and seek forgiveness. Likewise, be ready to forgive others who have wronged you. Holding onto grudges can block the flow of the Holy Spirit in your life. By confessing and forgiving, you create a clean slate, allowing the Holy Spirit to work freely within you.

9. Consistent Reflection on Life Choices: Regularly reflecting on the choices you make helps to align your life with the Holy Spirit's guidance. Take time to evaluate the decisions you have made and ask whether they reflect God's will. Seek the Holy Spirit's wisdom in making future decisions. This practice ensures that your actions and thoughts are in line with the direction God wants you to go.

It helps to keep your heart and mind aligned with God's purpose, maintaining a clear connection with the Holy Spirit.

10. Continual Learning: Commit to continual learning about the Holy Spirit and God's Word. Attend Bible studies, read spiritual books, listen to sermons, and seek knowledge that deepens your understanding of your faith. Learning keeps you engaged and motivated. It opens your mind to new perspectives and insights, helping you grow spiritually. The more you learn, the more you understand the Holy Spirit's role in your life, strengthening your connection and commitment.

11. Gratitude Practice: Cultivating a habit of gratitude keeps your heart open to the Holy Spirit. Regularly express thanks for the blessings in your life, both big and small, and shift your focus from what you lack to what you have. Gratitude invites the Holy Spirit to fill your heart with joy and contentment. Each day, take a moment to thank God for His presence and the work of the Holy Spirit in your life. This practice keeps your heart joyful and receptive to God's ongoing work.

12. Being Open to the Holy Spirit's Leading: Remaining open to the Holy Spirit's guidance requires a willing and flexible heart. Sometimes, the Holy Spirit may lead you in unexpected directions. Be willing to follow, even if it means stepping out of your comfort zone. Trust that the Holy Spirit knows what is best for you. This openness ensures that you are always in tune with God's will, ready to respond to His call. A willing heart keeps the connection with the Holy Spirit strong and active.

By incorporating these practical habits into your daily life, you can maintain a lasting connection with the Holy Spirit. These habits keep your faith strong and your heart attuned to God's presence.

Understanding the Eternal Perspective

Living a life of faith involves more than just our daily routines, challenges, and joys. It's about understanding that our journey on this earth is part of a much larger narrative, one that stretches beyond what we can see or experience in our everyday lives. As 2 Corinthians 4:18 reminds us, *"So we fix our eyes not on what is seen, but on what is unseen since what is seen is temporary, but what is unseen is eternal."* This is where the concept of an eternal perspective comes in, helping us to see the bigger picture of our faith journey.

What is the Eternal Perspective?

The eternal perspective is about seeing life through the lens of eternity. It's recognizing that our existence is not limited to the here and now but extends into the everlasting future that God has prepared for us. This perspective changes how we view our lives, our decisions, and even our struggles. It reminds us that our time on earth is temporary and there is a greater reality awaiting us. This understanding helps us to prioritize what truly matters and live with a sense of purpose and direction.

Why is the Eternal Perspective Important?

Grasping the eternal perspective gives meaning to our experiences. It provides a sense of hope, knowing that whatever we face in this life, it is not the end. There is more beyond this world, and that 'more' is filled with God's presence, peace, and joy. When we understand that our lives are part of an eternal plan, we can face hardships with courage, knowing that they are temporary and serve a greater purpose. This perspective encourages us to live in a way that aligns with God's will, focusing on what truly matters in the long run.

Seeing Beyond the Temporary

Life on earth is filled with temporary things—possessions, achievements, and even our physical bodies. These are important, but they are not the ultimate focus. The eternal perspective helps us see beyond these temporary aspects and focus on what will last forever. Relationships, love, kindness, and our relationship with God are eternal. By focusing on these, we invest in things that will have lasting value. When we keep eternity in mind, we are less likely to be consumed by the pursuit of temporary gains and more likely to invest in what has lasting significance.

How to Cultivate an Eternal Perspective in Daily Life

Living a life of faith involves more than just our daily routines, challenges, and joys. It's about understanding that our journey on this earth is part of a much larger narrative, one that stretches beyond what we can see or experience in our everyday lives.

Finding Peace in the Eternal Perspective

When we adopt an eternal perspective, we find peace amidst life's chaos. Knowing that our lives are in God's hands and that there is a plan beyond what we can see brings comfort. It helps us to trust that our struggles are temporary and that God is working everything out for our good. Romans 8:28 reminds us, *"And we know that in all things God works for the good of those who love him, who have been called according to his purpose."* This assurance helps us face trials with hope and courage.

1. Cultivating Patience and Perseverance: The eternal perspective teaches us patience. In a world where instant gratification is often the norm, it reminds us that God's timing is perfect. There may be delays, disappointments, and unanswered prayers, but with an eternal outlook, we learn to wait on the Lord. James 1:4 says, *"Let perseverance finish its work so that you may be mature and complete, not lacking anything."* Patience becomes a natural outcome when we trust that God's timing is part of His perfect plan for our lives.

2. Valuing Spiritual Growth Over Material Success: An eternal perspective shifts our focus from material success to spiritual growth. The world often measures success by wealth, status, or achievements. However, in God's eyes, true success is measured by the growth of our character, the depth of our faith, and the love we show to others. Jesus said in Matthew 6:19-21, *"Do not store up for yourselves treasures on earth, where moths and vermin destroy, and where thieves break in and steal. But store up for yourselves treasures in heaven."* By focusing on spiritual growth, we invest in treasures that will last for eternity.

3. Maintaining Integrity and Faithfulness: Living with an eternal perspective encourages integrity and faithfulness. Knowing that our actions have eternal consequences inspires us to live rightly, even when no one is watching. We are accountable to God for how we live our lives. Galatians 6:9 urges us, *"Let us not become weary in doing good, for at the proper time we will reap a harvest if we do not give up."* Understanding that God sees our faithfulness, even in small things, motivates us to stay true to our values.

4. Encouraging Generosity and Compassion: With an eternal perspective, we are more likely to be generous and compassionate. We understand that we are stewards of the resources God has given us, not owners. This mindset encourages us to share our blessings with others, knowing that acts of kindness and generosity reflect God's love. 2 Corinthians 9:6-7 reminds us, *"Whoever sows sparingly will also reap sparingly, and whoever sows generously will also* *reap generously."* Our generosity has an impact not only on those we help but also on our spiritual journey.

5. Finding Joy in Service: Serving others becomes a joy rather than a burden when viewed through the eternal perspective. Jesus taught that serving others is serving God. Matthew 25:40 says, *"Truly I tell you, whatever you did for one of the least of these brothers and sisters of mine, you did for me."* By serving, we are participating in God's work on earth, and this service will be remembered in eternity. This understanding brings joy and purpose to our actions.

6. Embracing Change with Hope: Change is inevitable, but with an eternal perspective, we can embrace it with hope. Life brings transitions—some planned, others unexpected. Understanding that God uses change to fulfill His purpose in our lives helps us to accept it with grace. Hebrews 13:8 provides comfort, *"Jesus Christ is the same yesterday and today and forever."* While circumstances change, God's promises remain constant, offering us stability and hope.

7. Strengthening Our Faith Through Community: An eternal perspective encourages us to build and be part of a faith community. Relationships with other believers provide support, encouragement, and accountability. Together, we can remind each other of the bigger picture and keep our focus on what truly matters. Hebrews 10:24-25 advises, *"And let us consider how we may spur one another on toward love and good deeds, not giving up meeting together, as some are in the habit of doing but encouraging one* *another."* A community rooted in eternal values helps to strengthen our faith.

Embracing the eternal perspective requires intentionality. It's about shifting our focus from the temporary concerns of daily life to the lasting promises of God. By doing so, we find peace, purpose, and joy that surpasses our understanding. We recognize that our lives are part of God's eternal plan, and each moment is an opportunity to align with His will.

Discovering and Embracing Your Role in God's Larger Plan

Each of us has a unique role in God's grand design. Understanding this role requires looking beyond our immediate desires and circumstances and recognizing that our lives are part of a larger story that God is writing. Embracing this perspective helps us see the significance of our actions and encourages us to live with purpose. Here's how to discover and embrace your role in God's plan, encouraging you to think beyond yourself.

1. Seek God's Guidance through Prayer: The first step in discovering your role in God's plan is to seek His guidance. Prayer is a powerful tool that opens our hearts and minds to God's direction. When we pray, we communicate with God, sharing our thoughts, fears, and hopes. It's also a time to listen. In the stillness of prayer, we can hear God's voice, guiding us toward our purpose. By seeking God's guidance through prayer, we position ourselves to understand the role He has for us.

2. Study for Clarity: Engaging with spiritual texts offers insights into God's character, promises, and plans. By regularly studying, we gain clarity on how to align our lives with God's will. Historical and scriptural examples show that God uses ordinary people to accomplish extraordinary things. These stories remind us that God has a role for each of us, no matter our background or circumstances. Through study, we learn what God values and how we can be a part of His work.

3: Reflect on Your Gifts and Talents: God has equipped each of us with unique gifts and talents. These abilities are not accidental; they are given for a purpose. Reflecting on what you are naturally good at can explain your role in God's plan. Whether you are gifted in teaching, serving, encouraging, or leading, embracing your strengths and using them to help others aligns with God's intentions. By recognizing and cultivating your talents, you actively participate in God's plan.

4: Be Open to God's Calling: Sometimes, God's plan for us may differ from our ideas or expectations. It's important to remain open to God's calling, even when it leads us in unexpected directions. God may place a desire in your heart to pursue a particular path, serve in a specific way, or support a cause. By being open to God's call, we show a willingness to be used for His purposes, trusting He knows what is best.

5: Engage with Your Community: Our role in God's plan is often connected to our relationships and interactions with others. Engaging with your community allows you to understand where your contributions are needed. Whether within your church, neighborhood, or workplace, building connections helps you see the opportunities to make a difference. By being present and involved, you can see how God might call you to act or serve, using your unique gifts for the good of others.

6: Pay Attention to the Needs Around You: God often reveals our roles through the needs we notice around us. If something stirs your heart or you feel a burden for a particular issue, it may indicate where God wants you to focus your efforts. You participate in God's work on earth by responding to these needs. By paying attention to these needs, you align your actions with God's heart.

7: Trust God's Timing: Discovering your role in God's plan may not happen overnight. It requires patience and trust in God's timing. There may be seasons of preparation where you feel uncertain about your direction. It's important to remain faithful and continue seeking God's guidance. Trust that God is at work, even when you don't see immediate results. Your faithfulness in the small things prepares you for the larger role God has for you.

8: Embrace Humility: Understanding our role in God's plan requires humility. It means recognizing that our lives are not just about personal success or comfort but about serving a greater purpose. Embracing humility allows us to put God's will above our own and serve others selflessly. It's about being willing to take the less glamorous roles if that's where God is calling us.

9: Be Willing to Make Sacrifices: Fulfilling your role in God's plan may require sacrifices. This could mean giving up time, resources, or personal ambitions to follow God's calling. Being willing to make sacrifices demonstrates our commitment to God's purpose. It shows that we value His plan more than our comfort, trusting that the rewards of following Him far outweigh the costs.

10: Encourage Others to Discover Their Role: Part of embracing your role in God's plan is helping others discover theirs. By encouraging and supporting others in their faith journey, you contribute to the larger picture of what God is doing. We are all interconnected, and our roles often complement each other. By helping others find and embrace their roles, you participate in building God's kingdom.

Discovering and embracing your role in God's larger plan requires a willingness to seek, listen, and act. It's about looking beyond yourself and recognizing that your life is part of a greater story. By aligning with God's will, using your gifts, and being open to His leading, you play a vital role in His work on earth. This brings purpose and meaning to your life, knowing you are contributing to something far greater than you can imagine.

Stories of People Finding Their Calling Through the Holy Spirit's Guidance

The journey of discovering one's calling can often be filled with uncertainty and doubt. However, stories of those who have found their calling through the Holy Spirit's guidance offer hope and inspiration. These individuals show that when we open our hearts to God's direction, we can find a purpose that brings joy and fulfillment.

1. Sarah's Journey to Impacting Lives:

Sarah had always enjoyed working with children, but she never saw herself as a teacher. After graduating from college, she pursued a career in business, believing it was the practical choice. Despite her success, Sarah felt a void in her life, a sense that something was missing. She started praying for clarity and direction, asking God to show her what He wanted for her life.

One Sunday, during a church service, Sarah felt a strong urge to volunteer for the children's ministry. Initially hesitant, she eventually decided to follow the prompting she felt in her heart. As she began working with the kids, Sarah discovered a deep passion for teaching. She felt a joy and fulfillment she had never experienced in her business career.

Encouraged by the joy she found in teaching, Sarah prayed for further guidance. The Holy Spirit continued to nudge her towards education. With faith and trust, she decided to leave her business career and pursue teaching full-time. Today, Sarah is a beloved elementary school teacher, impacting the lives of her students with kindness and love. She often shares that finding her calling through the Holy Spirit's guidance has been the most rewarding experience of her life.

2. David's Call to Serve Overseas:

David grew up in a small town and had never imagined traveling the world, let alone becoming a missionary. He was comfortable in his local church, involved in community activities, and had a stable job. However, during a mission trip organized by his church, David's heart was stirred. He saw the needs of people in other countries and felt a deep compassion for them.

After returning from the trip, David couldn't shake the feeling that God was calling him to serve overseas. He began to pray earnestly for direction. One night, while praying, David felt a deep sense of peace wash over him. He felt the Holy Spirit affirming his desire to become a missionary. Encouraged by this confirmation, David took a step of faith.

He began training with a mission organization and eventually moved to a country in need. David now works with a team to provide education, healthcare, and spiritual support to communities with little access to these resources. He often shares his testimony, saying, "The Holy Spirit led me to a place where my heart truly belongs. It's a life of service, where I've found my deepest fulfillment."

3. Maria's Shift to Helping Others Heal:

Maria was working in a high-pressure corporate job that demanded long hours and constant travel. Although her career was successful, Maria felt disconnected and exhausted. She began to question the meaning of her work and sought guidance through prayer and meditation on God's word. In her quiet times, Maria sensed the Holy Spirit, prompting her to use her listening skills and compassion to help others more directly.

Maria started volunteering at a local community center, offering to listen and support those going through difficult times. She found herself deeply moved by the stories she heard and realized how much she valued being there for others. The joy she experienced in these moments was undeniable. With time, Maria felt the Holy Spirit leading her toward a career in counseling.

After much prayer and consideration, Maria decided to pursue a degree in counseling. She left her corporate job and dedicated herself to helping others find healing and hope. Maria now works as a licensed counselor specializing in trauma recovery. She often shares that her new role feels less like a job and more like a calling. "The Holy Spirit guided me to a place where my skills and passions meet," Maria says. "I've found my purpose in helping others heal."

4. John's Journey to Sharing God's Message:

John had always loved writing but never saw it as more than a hobby. He worked in marketing, using his writing skills to promote products and services. However, John felt unfulfilled. He longed to write about deeper, more meaningful topics. He began to pray, asking the Holy Spirit to reveal how he could use his writing talents to serve God.

During a church retreat, John felt a strong conviction to start writing about faith. He sensed the Holy Spirit encouraging him to share his thoughts on spirituality, hope, and God's love. John began writing a blog, sharing personal reflections and insights he gained from his walk with God. His writing resonated with readers, many of whom reached out to thank him for the encouragement and hope his words brought them.

As his blog gained popularity, John felt called to write a book. With the guidance of the Holy Spirit, he published his first book, sharing stories of faith and redemption. Today, John is a full-time writer and speaker, using his platform to inspire others. He often says, "The Holy Spirit took my love for writing and turned it into a ministry. I'm grateful every day for the chance to share God's message through my words."

These stories exemplify that the Holy Spirit guides us toward our true calling when we remain open and seek God's direction. Whether teaching, serving, counseling, or writing, the Holy Spirit helps us find paths that bring us joy and align with God's purpose. By trusting in the Holy Spirit's guidance, we can discover our calling and live a life filled with meaning, hope, and fulfillment.

Living intentionally means waking up daily with purpose, knowing that our actions, words, and decisions matter. It's about seeking God's guidance in everything we do, from the smallest tasks to the biggest life choices. We open ourselves to His wisdom, direction, and strength by inviting the Holy Spirit into our daily lives. We allow God to work through us, using our unique gifts and talents to make a difference.

This partnership with the Holy Spirit is not just for special occasions or major life decisions; it is for every moment. It's in the kindness we show to others, the integrity we uphold, and the love we share. By committing to live intentionally, we become active participants in God's larger plan, contributing to a future filled with hope and purpose.

I challenge you to live each day with intention, partnering with the Holy Spirit to seek out and fulfill your calling. Ask God to reveal His plans for you, and be open to the opportunities He presents. Through this partnership, you will not only find your purpose but also create a life that is deeply fulfilling and impactful. Trust in the Holy Spirit, and take the step today toward a future that aligns with God's will.

Once again Janet has written a book from her heart. As she goes on her spiritual journey, she shares her insights and beliefs. A must read for anyone as they go on their journey.

Rob Kaercher, CIMA, AIF
Wealth Manager

I have had the honor of knowing Janet on a personal level. The testimony of her walk with our Lord Jesus Christ is evident in how she lives. Life With The Holy Spirit will equip the reader with the tools God has made available to all that seek its presents. Janet so eloquently shares the riches manifested as we chose to live by way of the Holy Spirit.

Lee Haney 8x Mr Olympia, Founder Of Lee Haney's Fitness & Games